Never Say *Whoa* in a Bad Place

by

Marilyn Pond

TEACH Services, Inc.
www.TEACHServices.com

**PRINTED IN
THE UNITED STATES OF AMERICA**

World rights reserved. This book or any portion thereof may not be copied or reproduced in any form or manner whatever, except as provided by law, without the written permission of the publisher, except by a reviewer who may quote brief passages in a review.

The author assumes full responsibility for the accuracy of all facts and quotations as cited in this book.

Copyright © 2010 TEACH Services, Inc.
ISBN-13: 978-1-57258-649-9
Library of Congress Control Number: 2010939444

Published by
TEACH Services, Inc.
www.TEACHServices.com

ACKNOWLEDGMENTS

I want to offer a heartfelt thanks to my uncles Frank, Lewis, and Clarence for providing added details to my dad's growing up years; to my cousins Delores, Janet, and Myrna for giving me family history details; to cousins Wilma (who was at the site of A Close Call and shared some new details) and Heather (who had recorded Dad's Wild Horses stories); to brother Lee and his wife for taking us to Little Horn Ranch and Potato Mountain (a part of Dad's life I missed while in Africa); and to Van for help with the story of Gypsy. You all helped me in my pursuit to retell these stories as accurately as possible.

In addition, I want to thank Billie Kouns for her helpful suggestions; my brother and sisters, whose stories are found in the section, Family Man; my husband, Doug, my chief encourager, advisor, and computer technician who cheerfully gave up several vacations to take me to the story sites to help me picture the settings; and the many others who have given me encouragement for this undertaking.

Contents

PART I: PRAIRIE BOY

Introduction		1
Chapter 1	Surprise!	3
Chapter 2	Early Carson Memories	6
Chapter 3	School Days	15
Chapter 4	New Horizons	28
Chapter 5	Northward Bound	36
Chapter 6	Almost Home	45
Chapter 7	Getting Started	51
Chapter 8	Forest Fires and Polka-Dot Pancakes	57
Chapter 9	Trapper and Farm Hand	65
Chapter 10	Riding the Rails	72
Chapter 11	A Good Trade	81
Chapter 12	Arrested	84
Chapter 13	Unexpected Company	88
Chapter 14	Greener Pastures	93

PART II: WILDERNESS MAN

Chapter 15	Lost	99
Chapter 16	Moving On	104
Chapter 17	Colporteur	109
Chapter 18	Niche Found	112
Chapter 19	Accident at Babine Lake	116
Chapter 20	A Brush with Death	121

Chapter 21   A Woolly Detour to Wild Horses 127
Chapter 22   A Found Stallion and a Lost Girl 134
Chapter 23   Finlay Forks Adventures 139
Chapter 24   Little Horn Ranch 157
Chapter 25   Coastal Adventures 163
Chapter 26   Retreaded 167
Chapter 27   Gypsy 172

PART III: FAMILY MAN

Conclusion   181
Chapter 28   There for Me 183
Chapter 29   Through the Wilderness 189
Chapter 30   Calm Amidst Storm 199
Chapter 31   The Rescue 201
Chapter 32   Lessons on Life 207
Chapter 33   My Knight in Blue Levis 213

Introduction

John's twin, Frank, says, "One thing about John, he always seemed to know what to do. No problem stumped him for long."

John just called it common sense.

Many who knew him agreed that this man of the wilderness had an uncommon amount of common sense.

He seemed at ease telling stories and flipping pancakes at a campfire, quieting a fussy toddler, sitting an unbroken horse, or batching in a tent all winter in the wilderness.

What do you do when you're lost? When the first-aid man at the sawmill faints at an accident? When a grizzly bear attacks? When you lose what you love?

Ask John, experienced woodsman, horseman, and family man.

For years, I encouraged him, and others, to write down or record the amazing adventures of this unassuming man—stories too good to be lost. Finally, I decided that if it were to happen, I needed to be the one to do it.

May you be inspired as you read the true-life stories of this remarkable man—my Dad!

PART I:
PRAIRIE BOY

Chapter One

Surprise!

Grandma Neufeld bustled about the house. Yes, everything was ready—the hot water, sheets and towels, string, and scissors. She made Mother as comfortable as possible, pulled up a chair to the bedside, and chatted quietly between the labor pains.

It was May 14, 1915, when she ushered me into the Goertzen home in Waldheim, Saskatchewan. Her skillful hands quickly took care of my needs as she announced, "You have another healthy son, Eva."

Mother gave a tired smile. "John Arthur."

Grandma Neufeld laid me in the basket and returned to Mother. "We have double duty tonight, dear. John Arthur has company."

My twin brother, Frankie, joined me three hours later, but I almost lost him then and there, because he just didn't want to take that first breath. Grandma Neufeld, a trained midwife from the old country, almost gave up on him.

"Please, try just once more!" begged Mother.

One more urgent spank, and Frankie was ready to let the whole world know that he had had enough of that.

We were numbers six and seven, joining Bill (eleven), Mary (nine), Herbert (eight), Diedrich (six) (for some reason, the spelling of this name alternated back and forth from one generation to the next in our culture), and Rueben (two) in the big yellow house in the prairie town of Waldheim.

Frankie was a bright little fellow. He soon could talk, but couldn't walk. I could walk, but couldn't talk. So he sat cross-legged on the floor for hours, telling me what to do. I was only too happy to oblige. It worked out so well for us, neither of us was in a hurry to mess the balance. But when we were both up and running, we must have been quite a handful. Our sister never knew where we would be next until she came up with the idea to tie us to opposite ends of a rope and then tie it to the washstand or table leg so she could wash the dishes or sweep the floor.

Just a little more than two years later, another set of twins arrived—Lewis and Leona. I remember a picture Mother had of all four of us twins sitting on her knees. She was a very loving mother, but when someone once asked her what she did when she found out she had another set of twins, she said, "I cried!"

Father always hired a girl to help Mother for the first few weeks after a new baby arrived. And Mary was a big help.

"Please let me stay home and help Mother with the babies," she begged.

Surprise!

"But don't you want to be a teacher?" asked Father.

"I can still be a teacher," Mary insisted. "I have lots of time."

And so it was that Mary missed two years of school for us. No wonder we always had a special tie.

At six months of age, beautiful little Leona got sick. The family doctor came to see her, and he gave her some new medicine that was supposed to be really good. Leona went to sleep right away . . . but she never woke up.

Of course, I only remember that because of the stories Mother told us later on.

Chapter Two

Early Carson Memories

When Frankie and I were still very little, our family moved to a farm near the tiny rural town of Carson, just a few miles from Waldheim. Father thought the farm would be a much better place for a growing family of boys, and he bought two quarter-sections of land about a mile south of the North Saskatchewan River.

Father, Dietrich Goertzen, was a handsome, likeable man; Mother was cheerful and open. She liked to sing while she worked. Early in the morning, she would whistle while she lit the fire in the cookstove and got the big porridge pot heating for breakfast.

They both spoke the Low German dialect (Plauttdeutsch) and were of Mennonite stock. Their parents had immigrated to the United States to avoid persecution in Russia where their families were farming by invitation of Queen Katherine. She had given the colony a large fertile plain of about 300,000 acres east of the Molotschna River and north of the Sea of Azov (now part of the Ukraine) in the early 1800s. The hard-working, peace-loving Mennonites prospered and settled many villages—sort of a state within a state. But around 1870, new laws were passed in St. Petersburg, which took away their special privileges, including their own education system and military exemption. They were given ten years to adjust.

So it was that hundreds of families sold their goods and left their towns and villages over the next ten years to start a new life in America.

Our Neufelds, together with a number of other families, crossed Europe by train to Belgium, where they boarded the ship "State of Nevada." This was no luxury cruise ship; they traveled steerage class and sailed into New York City on August 5, 1875, with not much more than the shirts on their backs. Once through immigration, some of the families homesteaded in North Dakota. Mother was born in 1883. When she was ten, her family moved to Saskatchewan and helped found the town of Waldheim (home in the woods).

Father came to Canada later as a young man of twenty-four. He was looking for work and was hired as a clerk at the Neufeld's hardware store in the winter of 1899. Father knew a good thing when he saw it, so he married a prize—the owner's daughter, my mother, Eva—in 1902. She was nineteen, and Father was twenty-seven. Around the time my brother Rueben was born, they attended some tent meetings, and along with a number of other Mennonites, they joined the Seventh-day Adventist Church. In fact, two of my uncles, D.D. and John Neufeld, became Adventist ministers.

That's my roots in a nutshell.

Sometimes the teachers in our little prairie schools were single ladies, and they would board in people's homes. Miss Tunna was one of these. She was Mary's teacher, and she stayed in our home. On visitors' day, Mary put on our Sabbath best and took Frankie and me to school as her "guests." That was a big thing for us at four years of age, and it is one of my earliest memories. We were given crayons and paper, and we felt very privileged.

By this time, our world was expanding. We loved to accompany our older brothers to the barn and entertain ourselves while they did chores.

We knew we were supposed to stay inside the fence, but I knew that there was a wonderful, big world out there just waiting to be explored. One time when we were close to the fence, I put my finger to my lips and said, "Shhh."

We looked around. No one was in sight. Under the fence we scrambled.

Running through the tall grass, I suddenly found myself plunging down an old well. Fortunately, instead of water there was mud at the bottom, and I landed without much damage. I picked myself up and looked up the fifteen or so feet to the opening just in time to see Frankie's face anxiously peering over the edge before he lost his balance. Luckily for both of us, the old board he grabbed on to held. His frantic cries brought Bill running to the rescue. He plucked Frankie off the board, and then ran for a rope to fish me out.

I put the loop under my armpits like he told me, and soon I was back up in the sunshine, but to this day I keep a cautious lookout for old wells when walking through overgrown property.

Another time, we were having a wonderful time playing on a fresh load of hay, so fresh, in fact, that it was still on the wagon in front of the barn. Now, a haystack is one of the most fun places to play! We jumped in it, dug in it, and slid down it, hollering and having the time of our lives.

"Watch me," Frank called, as he slid down the other side. The trouble was that it offset a bunch of hay that carried him right off of the rack.

I climbed up and over to see, but I couldn't find him. I heard a faint call, "Help!"

There was Frank, dangling between the hayrack and the barn wall.

"I'm coming," I shouted, as I hastily scrambled off the wagon and ran to his aid. But he hung out of reach, and I ran screaming toward the house, "Help! Help! Frank is hung."

Herbert heard the call and came to Frank's rescue.

Sometimes Mother would let Bill take us to the slough just north of our quarter to go swimming. No one around there had heard of swimming trunks, so we didn't miss them a bit. The water felt cool and wet, just like water should. That's where I had my first swimming lesson.

Even as a youngster, I was attracted to horses. Galloping around the yard on my stick, I would lustily sing:

"Hopp, hopp, hopp, Pferdchen lauf galopp.
"Uber stock und uber steine,
"aber brich dir nicht die Beine.
"Hopp, hopp, hopp, Pferdchen lauf galopp."

This roughly translated to:
"Clip-clop, clip-clop, clip-clop, the pony trots,
"Over sticks and over stones,
"But he does not break his (bones),
"Clip-clop, clip-clop, clip-clop, the pony trots."

Never Say Whoa In A Bad Place

I grew up around and on horses. Father liked beautiful, spirited horses. Back in those days, horses were a status symbol. To drive a nicely matched team of horses compared to driving a snazzy pickup truck or a sports car today. And he gave us boys an early start on them. But I think I was the most head-over-heels in love with them.

Of course, it wasn't all play and no work. A job I could do when still quite small was to herd the cows in spring or between harvests to give their pasture a break. Mother packed a lunch for me in a syrup pail, and feeling very grown up, I would climb a fence to get up on Minnie's back. She was a quiet, reliable horse. My job was to keep the cows from straying into the fields that had not been harvested yet. I did not dare climb down, even to go to the bathroom, since there were no fences to help me climb back up. Of course, this was not a major problem. I would just swing both legs to one side and do my business. It worked. I loved that job, because it put me on a horse.

Father also let me help him with the harrowing. It made the fields look like they had been combed. I liked that. He wouldn't let me help with the disking; he said that was too dangerous. But probably the job I was most proud of during my preschool years was hauling grain to the elevators in Hepburn. Father must have had a lot of confidence in me, because he let me drive our work-team, Dick and Fanny, the eight miles to Hepburn all by myself. And I wasn't about to disappoint him.

One day Father brought home a new dog.

"This is a special dog," he informed us. "He is a born and trained herd-dog."

I can still see Rover. He had a short tail, spots, and a sideways trot. Somehow, his initial behavior did not win Father's confidence, so he kept Rover tied up for a few days to settle him down and let him get used to us. The day came when Father decided to try Rover out on the calves. I went along to watch.

The instant the dog was released, he was off. He chased those calves around and around the field.

Father called and whistled and shouted in vain. This was the life for Rover, and he was not about to stop. Father finally grabbed a chain and waited for the calves and Rover on their next round. The calves streaked past, and Father stood waiting, chain held high. I closed my eyes tight, but I still heard the "Wham!"

I opened my eyes. Rover was on his back; he kicked his legs and then lay still. I thought things were over for Rover, but they weren't. After that, when Father said "Whoa," he never had to say it twice for Rover.

An annual highlight each fall was the arrival of a train from British Columbia (BC) with carloads of apples. Several large bins were left at Hepburn, and the farmers came from miles around to help themselves to two or three sacks full of apples. When Father returned home with our share, we were allowed to eat all the apples we wanted the first evening—lovely crisp, juicy apples. What a treat!

The next day, Mother and Mary would sort out the best of the fruit to save and ration. Soon after, I could smell spicy apple pies baking. The rest of the fruit was turned into applesauce and preserved.

Christmas Day was always a day to remember.

"Chore time! Time to get up," would come the call.

All was dark as night outside, but what a scrambling as we remembered it was Christmas morning. As quickly as possible, the cows were milked, the animals fed, and breakfast was eaten. Dad and Bill would harness Rock and Floss and Daze and Dolly if the snow was really deep, hitching them to the bobsled. We would all pile in, snuggled under warm wool quilts with heated rocks at our feet, and set off for Grandpa and Grandma Neufeld's house in Waldheim, twelve miles away. Mother would lead us in singing Christmas carols. It was all so jolly.

Aunts, uncles, and cousins were all there to add to the excitement. We children were shooed outdoors to play fox-and-goose in the snow or to climb the hayloft, while the women set to work in the kitchen. Roasted chickens, a stuffed goose, piles of fluffy mashed potatoes, gravy, pies, paipe naete (peppernuts), and other wonders took place before we finally heard the dinner bell.

As soon as we were scrubbed clean, we children took our place on the stairs to wait for the adults to eat first. It smelled and looked so good, and everyone ate so heartily, it seemed nothing would be left for us. But Grandma always reserved plenty of food in the kitchen for the "kindt," and yes, our turn always came. (This was never thought of as mean. We had very kind parents and grandparents. It was just the way things were done.)

After dinner came the program: Grandfather's speech, then recitations, skits, and songs prepared by the different families. Tall fathers stood in the back against the walls, the mothers sat in front of them, and the children sat on the floor and stairs. Finally Grandmother's turn came. She handed out the gifts—a paper bag filled with treats for each of us children and a hanky or something for each adult.

Just a few weeks before I turned six, Grandma Neufeld came with her little satchel to stay at our place. We boys all had to go to the Brucks', our neighbors, for the night. When we got back the next morning, there was little Clarence all wrapped up sleeping in a basket. Our big gray cat was sitting up on the basket, just purring away at the baby. Three-and-a-half-year-old Lewis said, "I bet Kitty thinks it's a tiger."

I don't know how he came up with that idea, but it tickled my funny bone enough that I never forgot it. That summer I sure enjoyed pushing little Clarence around in his buggy up and down our long tree-lined lane to the road. I also got to pick wild strawberries with Diedrich in our south quarter, which was mostly just wild pasture.

Clarence was only a few months old when the plague of diphtheria hit the prairies. Hardly a family was missed. Fortunately, babies under six months seem to have a natural immunity, so Clarence didn't even get sick. Diedrich, Frank, and I were hit hard. The doctor was busy day and night, riding from one farm to the next—I don't know how he did it. One of the things that happens with this disease is the growth of kind of a membrane that closes off your throat so you can't breathe.

The doctor swabbed my throat with a goose feather dipped in coal oil. Ugh! It was terrible. When thirteen-year-old Diedrich died, Frank thought for sure he was next. He had just gotten a new pair of shoes before he got sick, and he asked our parents to please give his new shoes to Johnny. I was too sick to even know or care, but we both pulled through. I must have been pretty sick, for it was many months before I could walk again. It felt strange to have Father and Mother carry me around. Although we were six, we did not go to school that year.

Father liked to say, "I have one and a half dozen boys, and each one has a favorite sister. On the occasions we were all home, there were ten of us; at harvesttime there were even more of us with the hired hands. Mealtimes were always jolly. We had lots to eat from Mother's ample garden. Unexpected company? No problem. Mother would hurry out to the henhouse to fetch a chicken for the dumplings.

Never Say Whoa In A Bad Place

Suppers were light and simple. A favorite was glumps (fresh cottage cheese with a little homemade jam stirred in) and prips (our homemade wheat coffee). Friday evening suppers consisted of prips and broot (bread). This simple supper was necessary after a very busy preparation day of cleaning the house, preparing a special Sabbath dinner, and giving everyone a turn to bath in the washtub.

The years quickly slipped by. Before I knew it, it was time for Frankie and me to start school. What new adventures awaited us?

Chapter Three

School Days

The sun was barely up when we heard Mother call, "Boys!" This was the big day. Mother had laid out freshly ironed white shirts and our Sabbath ties on top of our knickers and socks. We would look our very best for our first day of school.

I felt butterflies in my tummy. I was sure glad big brother Rueben was there for us. We had been practicing our English all summer with Mary's help, before she and Herbert left for boarding school in North Battleford. We knew Mr. Harder, our teacher, from church. In fact, they had invited us over for dinner one Sabbath, where we were introduced to cooked greens, and were expected to play with his daughters, Josephine and Irene. I decided they must be very rich because Mrs. Harder had a fur coat.

All these things swirled around in my mind as we walked to school that morning.

Actually, school turned out to be quite pleasant. I learned more English, how to read, and how to add and subtract. Frank really took to learning. Even in first grade, he wrote a love letter to a pretty little girl that made me blush.

Recess was my favorite subject for sure. We would play Pump Pump, Pull Away, Tag, and games that required more imagination, such as pretending to take grain to the elevator. I didn't mind at all whether my team of "horses" were boys or girls, although some boys thought this was a big thing. Or we would simply play Horses. Once, when I was the horse, I made the mistake of licking some beautiful hoarfrost off the wire fence, and I promptly left a strip of my tongue behind on the wire. I thought twice about sticking my tongue on things after that.

One of the most important school events of the year for the whole community was the Christmas concert. We practiced our poems, songs, dialogues, and skits for weeks. On the day of the concert, desks were shoved against the walls, benches set up, and decorations hung.

The room was packed for the concert, and all the children dressed in their Sabbath-best. It was pretty exciting. And after the performance, we all received a reward from the school board, even the preschoolers—a bag of peanuts and candy, and maybe even an orange, a rare treat indeed.

An annual school event that stands out even above the Christmas concert was the drive for gopher control. These little rodents damaged farmers' crops and ruined pastureland. Their holes put horses at risk for breaking a leg if they stepped in unawares. Mr. Ebeck, the municipal reeve, would pay the school two or three cents a tail. This money went to buy sports supplies—baseballs, bats, and footballs (soccer balls). The school would take off an entire day, divide the students into about four teams, then scatter to see which team would come up with the most gopher tails by the end of the day.

In our area, there were three different kinds of gophers: the prairie gophers, bush gophers, and striped gophers. Each kind had habits that helped determine how to catch them. For instance, the prairie gopher lives in a gopher village or "town." Its network of underground tunnels has several entrances or exits. The bush gopher is easily recognized by its bushy tail; the striped gopher by its stripe. These make homes with only one entrance, so they are easier to catch. All of them tended to live in fields near bushy areas that often had a slough or puddle. This was important, for water was a chief weapon.

Most farm boys had plenty of tricks up their sleeves. We worked in pairs, one armed with a bucket of water, the other with a pointed stick. It was not a good day for the gophers, but it helped hold them in check for the farmers, and it benefited the school.

Although he was a stern teacher, I remember Mr. Harder bragging about me once. "Put John on a horse, and he's at home."

That made me feel good inside.

He could also draw well, and he enjoyed teaching art. But he was willing to use this talent in other ways too. On learning that Mother's chickens needed a new henhouse, he drew up plans for the fanciest chicken coop I had ever seen. Father and the older boys actually built it, making our chickens definitely upper class, although I don't think they realized how lucky they were.

Mr. Harder taught me in first and second grade, but there is only one particular lesson that stands out in my mind from second grade. It must have been very important, for the boys were separated from the girls, and we took turns playing outside while the other group had their special lesson. "Don't play with satchel organs" is the point I got from it all. I was mystified. My sister Mary had a small organ. She didn't have a satchel for it, but she even took it to church and played it there. I really wanted to ask Mr. Harder what was wrong with them, but the older boys were acting very uncomfortable, and the teacher looked so stern. So I tried to look very wise and gravely nodded my head.

That was my only formal instruction in sex education, but I didn't know for several years what "satchel organs" he was talking about.

At the end of the school day, there was always a race to see who could get their horses out of the schoolyard first. With three of us boys working together, we could harness and hitch up pretty fast. Even though we were in the younger set, we certainly weren't the last ones out. I saw more than one sleigh tip over in the ditch in the mad scramble to win.

Summer holidays were very busy times on the farm for the grown-ups and older children. Frank, Lewis, and I had our usual chores. I enjoyed milking Betsy in the evening. She was an easy milker, and it made me feel proud to get a full bucket of rich milk. There were chickens to feed and water, eggs to gather, cows to herd, butter to churn, and errands to run.

If "all work and no play makes Jack a dull boy," I don't know. We brothers sure knew how to play. The lack of store-bought toys didn't slow us down a bit. Playing Indians was a favorite pastime. We made teepees with willows and bows from poplars. Arrows were sharpened sticks or sometimes nails. We'd draw a line in the dirt, and if anyone from either tribe crossed the line, the battle was on!

School Days

One time, Rueben decided to try out a new bow and arrow he had just made. He aimed at a heifer and hit his mark. We got to see how well a heifer can buck until the "arrow" fell off. That was a little too rough!

We still liked swimming in the slough, and sometimes at night Bill would take us to Brucks' dugout to swim. They didn't mind, as it was just used to water their cattle. (Our big brother had some ulterior motives, I believe, for he eventually married Hilda, their pretty dark-haired daughter.) I actually liked swimming at night. The air was cooler, which made the water feel warmer, and I liked watching the lightning. On the prairies, the sky is a big part of the scenery, and in the summer, lightning plays in the sky a lot.

But most of our free hours were spent playing "farm." Rueben coached us along if he had spare time. We painstakingly tied string on small posts for fences. Cotton fluff from weeds covered our wooden sheep. Our horses were wooden spools with nails for legs, heads, and tails. Houses and barns were included. Our tractors were wooden blocks with carefully carved wheels that actually turned on axles. Rueben helped us extract the gears from an old clock, and he attached them to one of our tractors so that it made a noise like a motor when we pushed it along. These farms were set up rather permanently just behind the rows of spruce trees lining the south side of our driveway. It was hard to leave our play sometimes.

One way Father encouraged instant obedience when he called, "Boys!" was to invite the first two boys to reach him to climb into the wagon with him if he was going to town. The storekeeper at the Hepburn Trading Company always had a barrel of hard candies for children who visited the store to dip into. Even better than the candies were the times Father let me drive his team.

Third Grade

All too soon, summer was past, and I found myself back at school. Mr. Harder was gone, and our new teacher, Mr. Hirtz[1], was even more stern. I am sure it was no easy task to teach eight grades of forty to fifty children.

Somehow, I got off on the wrong foot early in third grade arithmetic. Gone were the days of adding and subtracting, which I was really good at. I could memorize, so multiplication wasn't all that bad, but about that time, all four of us Goertzen boys who were in school came down with the mumps at the same time, and were we sick!

They say that misery likes company—well, we had it: Rueben, Frank, Lewis, and me. Mother gently nursed us through the nasty stage of fever and headache. As we started to feel better, strangely, we looked worse. If we could have laughed, we would have to see ourselves with protruding jowls and lumpy necks. We were certainly getting into better spirits, and Mother decided that she and little Clarence could go to town with Father for the day. Rueben was left in charge of the rest of us.

We were in our bedroom quietly entertaining ourselves when Rueben gave a whoop that made me jump—Rueben, the quiet one!

"Listen to this," he said, and started reading. "Not only are onions useful for their flavor. They have many healing properties. They can be used in poultices and cough syrups, and are particularly medicinal when used raw, speeding recovery from colds, influenza, mumps . . ."

He stopped and looked at us. We looked at him and then at each other, and then up at the ceiling.

I figured we were all thinking of the same thing—Mother's big cache of onions in the attic. After harvesting and curing a bumper crop, we boys had hauled those bundles of heavy onions up the stairs

---

1   Name changed

and through the hole in the ceiling. There we spread them carefully so they would stay dry. The warmth from the rooms below kept them from freezing. It was Mother's winter supply, but there was more than enough.

"What are we waiting for?" I asked.

Obviously nothing. We had a ladder up to that hole and the trap door open before you could say "Jack Robinson."

We sat down, and each of us selected an onion, peeled back the pungent skins, and bit in. Oh, these were no mild, sweet onions; these were full-power, he-man quality onions. But I tell you, we kept eating. Tears were running down our cheeks, but that wasn't about to stop us.

I don't remember us getting well right away, but I'm sure we all had clear sinuses after that.

Once we got better and were back at school again, we were heavy into long division. Perhaps it had been introduced while I was at home with the mumps, or perhaps my mind had been out somewhere with the horses. Whatever the case, I didn't get it.

Mr. Hirtz would send the third graders to the blackboard. "Nineteen thousand seven hundred thirty-six divided by forty-five," he might say, and then he would carry on working with another grade.

We would transcribe the problem onto the board and set to work. Too soon, my buddies were finished, hiding their answers behind their chalk brushes. The teacher would return and check their answers. They would then erase their answers and return to their desks. More often than not, I found myself alone at the board, a distinctly uncomfortable situation. I would try this and that, from every angle I could think of. Embarrassed and scared, my thinking was more muddled than ever. I learned how it felt to be the class klutz.

In frustration, Mr. Hirtz would push my face into the board. Even that close to the problem, I still didn't get it. If anything, my mental block grew bigger.

What a relief when recess finally rolled around. I could get out in the fresh, cold air, line up my team of "horses" and run and laugh and have fun.

The Fight

"John is a sissy. He has girl horses," I heard Jacob chant in a sing-song voice.

Who cares? I thought. I ignored him and kept on driving my team. He jumped in front of my team and repeated his chant with a little dance. I couldn't maneuver around him.

"Look here," I said. "Our Daisy and Dolly can outwork any horses your Father has, and they're girls, so move!"

"Make me!" he challenged.

By this time I was warming up, but I turned my team and clicked my tongue for them to keep going.

"See, John is a sissy," Jake shouted. "Too scared to fight."

I had had it. "You know we're not allowed to fight on the school grounds. If you really want to fight, wait for me on the road after school," I told him.

The bell rang, and we all lined up and went in for afternoon classes. I couldn't concentrate on my schoolwork. Whatever had I gotten myself into? Jacob was bigger than I, and he was a much better fighter, I was sure. Although I had plenty of brothers, fighting was not an acceptable option in our home.

Surely, Jacob was just bluffing. Or maybe he'd forget. But then again, I'd better be ready for the worst. If it came to that, I decided, I would give him all I had.

The afternoon dragged by. Finally, Mr. Hirtz said, "Put your books away."

School Days

Suddenly, the afternoon had gone by too quickly. I glanced Jacob's way. He was looking at me. I glanced away.

I was one of the last ones out of the schoolhouse, and my boots felt like lead as I made my way to the stables. I fiddled with the harness strap, trying to kill some time. Maybe Jacob would get tired of waiting for me.

"Come on, John. What's the hold-up?" asked Rueben.

"He's going to have a fight with Jacob Enns," piped up Lewis.

"He is WHAT?" asked Rueben in surprise. He had not seen the incident on the playground, so Frank and Lewis filled him in on the details, as I wasn't up to much talking right then.

By this time, we were heading out of the school grounds. In seconds, I would know if I was on.

Sure enough, there up ahead was Jacob, standing in the middle of the road. Suddenly I felt heat rising up my neck. We drove a bit closer.

"Stop here," I told Rueben.

"Are you sure?" he asked hesitantly.

"Well, I guess I got myself into this. I better see it through."

I jumped off the sled, took off my jacket, and walked out to meet Jacob. My brothers will vouch for me that I let him make the first swing. Then I let go with everything I had. It was over so fast I couldn't believe it. Neither could Jacob, I'm sure.

But it wasn't over. The next day, Jacob came to school with two black shiners.

"What happened?" was the big question whispered around.

Jacob wasn't telling, and I certainly wasn't, even if the fight didn't happen on the school grounds. But I think some of the kids put two and two together, and I think Mr. Hirtz had a sneaking suspicion, which may have had some bearing on what happened several weeks later, but that's another story.

The Snowball

"John Arthur Goertzen!"

My laughter died in my throat as our angry teacher stormed around the corner of the schoolhouse, bellowing my name.

"Did you throw that snowball, young man?"

The rest of the children melted back as I stood rooted to the snowy ground, shaking in my boots. Mr. Hirtz had a red welt on his cheek, and snow still clung to his collar. Someone had nailed him good.

"No, sir, I was right here." Nervous, I dropped the snowball I had in my hand for the snow fort we were building before realizing how guilty that action probably made me look.

His eyes narrowed. "Then why were you laughing as I came around the corner just now?"

My mind raced, but I couldn't think of anything to say that would convince him. My friends shuffled miserably, and I heard someone start to cry as Mr. Hirtz clamped onto the back of my neck and marched me around to the schoolhouse door. As I stumbled up the steps, I tried once more. "Honest, Mr. Hirtz, I didn't do it."

"Take off your coat and lean over your desk." He reached for his razor strap.

The strapping I received that day—for something I hadn't done—was so severe that I could not sit for several days. At the age of 9, my parents decided not to send me back to school. I gladly complied.

While my brothers—Rueben, Frank, Lewis and, later, Clarence—continued their schooling, I happily stayed home to help Father on the farm or Mother in the house. It was right about this time that Mother gave birth to our last little brother, Don. My formal education was over, but I sure had a lot more learning to do.

"How'd you like to join me today on my trapline run?" asked Bill.

Bill was the oldest of the nine of us. He was already grown up—he was twenty. During most of the year he worked for farmers in the area, but during the winter he ran a trapline.

Bill knew how to do almost anything. I felt very privileged and grown up as we got our packs ready and set out.

We headed down toward the North Saskatchewan River where there were a lot of wooded areas. I watched carefully as he showed me how to set up willow snares in brush for rabbits. We worked our way down toward the river and then back up again to the sloughs, where he showed me how to break the ice and set snares in the water for the ever-abundant muskrats. Next, I watched as he carefully skinned a few rabbits, avoiding any rips so he could get prime price.

"Are you ready to give it a try?" Bill asked, handing me his knife.

"I'm game."

I took the knife and slit around the feet, made the undercut, and carefully peeled back the fur. I held it up for inspection.

Bill looked it over. "Perfect. How'd you like to be my partner?"

We shook hands on the deal.

After a couple of winters working with Bill, I set up my own trapline. Of course, the money went to the family pot, but once in a while I spotted something in the Eaton's catalogue that I really wanted. I particularly remember a package with three masks—an Indian chief, a pirate, and a kewpie doll—for twenty-five cents. I was sure I could put such things to good use. Imagine my surprise when Mother agreed to let me order them.

When my package arrived, I squirreled it away in our bedroom, with only Frank in the know.

"Don't tell anyone," I said.

A few nights later our folks went over to visit the neighbors. Now was my chance. I chose the smiling, rosy-cheeked kewpie doll mask to surprise my dark, handsome but shy brother, Rueben. Putting it on, I checked in the little mirror on our wall and was quite impressed with the effect. I slipped downstairs and out the front door.

Knock, knock. I stepped back and waited expectantly.

The door opened, but it was Frank, and he had already seen my masks. But by the way the light was shining from the coal-oil lamp above Frank's head, I figured that Reuben was just behind the door, ready to give moral support to Frank if need be, for a knock on the door at night was a rare thing for us.

If my prank was going to work, I had to act fast. Pushing past Frank, I stuck my head around the door with my new round, smiling face. What a huge mistake that was! My shy brother, startled out of his wits, let loose a reflex swing with his one free hand that shattered my false face to smithereens and sent blood pouring from my injured nose.

While Frank ran to get some water and rags to stop the bleeding and clean up the mess on the floor, Reuben scrambled to pick up the pieces, apologizing over and over. But nothing could put my kewpie-doll face together again.

This proved to be a valuable lesson that I would need to review once or twice—I'd better think twice before playing jokes, because they just might backfire.

The spring that I turned twelve, our church got involved in a Temperance Campaign. You don't hear much about temperance anymore, but the idea was to discourage smoking and drinking. The church had received a whole pile of the non-smoking edition of Our Little Friend magazines to sell. I volunteered to help sell the magazines. After all, it was for a good cause, and it would serve as a little business venture for the church.

Father actually took off a day, even though it was such a busy time for farmers, to help me get started. I was to visit each farm in the whole area and sell the magazines, five cents apiece.

The project took me several weeks, and I really enjoyed talking to people. Most of them were friendly, or at least polite, and my pile of magazines got smaller and smaller. Riding Minnie, I worked my way farther and farther from home.

One day, I saw a farmer and his son plowing a field. I turned off the road to talk to them.

"What are you selling?" the farmer asked, stopping his horse and coming to meet me.

"Temperance magazines," I told him, pulling one out of my sack. "They're full of lots of good things about staying healthy. And they cost only five cents apiece."

"Let's see a couple of them," he said.

I obliged.

By this time, his son had joined him. The father handed one of the magazines to his son. They went over to the edge of the field, sat down on a log, and proceeded to read through the whole magazine while I politely waited. When the father finished the last page, he got up and handed the magazine back to me with a curt, "No thanks," and headed back to his waiting horse. The son sheepishly followed suit.

My jaw must have dropped. How lowdown can a fellow get? I wondered, as I tucked the two read papers back into my bag and turned back to the road.

In the end, I felt like I had really accomplished something worthwhile when my stack of papers were all gone. And I had learned a little about salesmanship.

Chapter Four

New Horizons

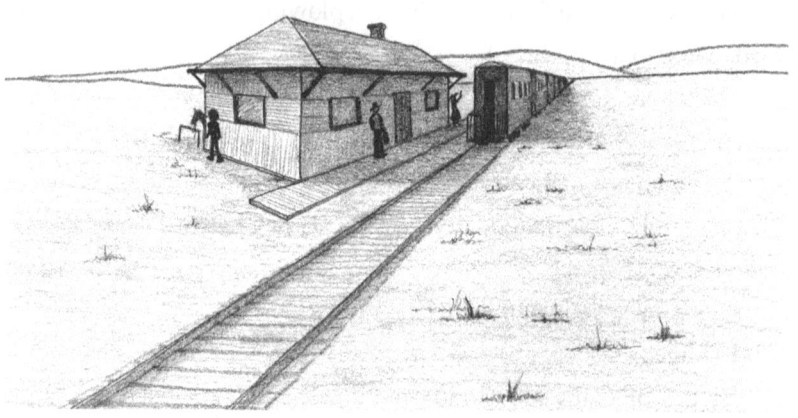

"Hey, John, did you forget that we get to go to John Dairy's today?" Frank, my twin, reminded me. "Let's hurry."

I stepped up my speed cleaning out the stalls. I enjoyed the excursion to visit the old shoemaker. The Yankee bachelor always seemed glad to see us Goertzen boys, and while fixing our shoes, he would tell us exciting stories. We were too big now to use his bed for a trampoline, but we still loved his flapjacks and the way he would flip them high in the air to turn them, catching them neatly back in the heavy black skillet.

Soon we had fresh bedding on the floors and hay in the mangers ready for the evening.

With his sharp pocketknife, Frank cut out a chunk of leather from an old work collar and headed to the house to pick up the worn-out shoes. At the same time, I grabbed a halter and a handful of oats and headed for the pasture. Minnie saw me about the same time I spotted her. She whinnied and trotted over to the gate. I gave her the oats, scratched her head, slipped on the halter, and led her out through the gate. With a little jump, I boosted myself up on her bare back and rode up to the house for Frank.

What a day! Summer was beautiful on the prairies. Our farm was near Carson, just about eight miles from Hepburn. With the wind in my face, the huge dome of a sky above, and a horse under me, all was right with my world.

John Dairy lived with his dog in a tarpaper shack close to the North Saskatchewan River. It took us a few hours of riding to get there. As we neared his home, we could see him plowing the field with his horse. When he spotted us, he immediately stopped the horse and came over to see what we wanted.

"I needed a break anyway," he said with a twinkle in his eyes.

"You good man," said Frank. It sounds a little strange in English, but that was a very polite thing to say in the Low German dialect we spoke at home.

We waited for Mr. Dairy to get his horse, and then we followed him to his shack.

"You must be hungry after that long ride. Let me fix up some flapjacks," he said, adding dry wood to the hot coals in his cookstove.

We smiled in anticipation while he wiped out a dirty mixing bowl and poured in water, flour, a little sugar, and baking powder. Soon the hotcakes were sizzling, and he was telling all about Shep's latest escapade with the coyotes.

"You should have seen how smart those coyotes worked. The

one had Shep way out past the barn, while her mate moved in from behind so he couldn't get back to the house. Lucky thing I was there or Shep would have been breakfast." He gave the last flapjack an extra hard flip so it turned twice before landing neatly on the piled high plate.

While we downed the flapjacks and Roger's Syrup, John patched the soles of our shoes, finishing with a quick polish.

"Wow, Mr. Dairy, they look like new," I told him. "Thank you!"

Frank pulled out a quarter from his pocket for payment. Then we mounted Minnie and headed for home. We rode in silence for a while. I was thinking about our big, happy family and John Dairy with only Shep. I guess Frank was too.

"He must get awful lonely," Frank said quietly.

Man of the House

Excitement was in the air. I could detect a strange light in Father's eye. I caught snatches of long, low conversations at night between him and Mother. "Cheap land . . . good for our boys . . . chance of a lifetime."

I was turning these things over in my twelve-year-old mind, trying to decide what it all meant. It sounded like adventure, and that was something I was always ready for.

One morning after milking the two cows, letting the hens out, feeding and grooming the horses, and cleaning out the stalls, we boys made a race for the house to scrub up for breakfast.

Mmm . . . I could smell fresh biscuits even before I opened the door. Mary had made them, I was sure. She and Herb were home from boarding school at North Battleford.

Herb had just graduated and was home for a brief visit before heading to Manitoba to earn money for college. Mary still had a couple years to make up from when she stayed home to help Mother with us twins. It was so good to be a whole family again.

No time to dally. We lined up at the washbasin and slid into our places as quickly as we could.

Father proudly surveyed his family, from twenty-three-year-old Bill to three-year-old Don, and then said, "Let's pray together."

We all bowed our heads. "Kom Herr Jesus, sie unser gast (Come, Lord Jesus, be our guest) . . . Amen." We prayed the familiar German words in unison.

Father looked at Mother with a question mark on his face. She nodded.

He cleared his throat for our attention. "What would you think about going homesteading?"

Everything broke loose.

"Where to?"

"What about school?"

"How'd we get there?"

"What about my kitties?"

I finally found my voice. "When can we go?"

"Wait, wait," said Father with a laugh. "One at a time, please."

Breakfast was all but forgotten as Father told how the Canadian government was encouraging farmers to settle farther north by offering new land for almost nothing in exchange for clearing and farming part of it.

He answered our questions as best he could. "It would mean a lot of hard work and roughing it for a few years," he warned us. "Are you willing?"

Oh, yes. We were willing.

So it was that Father, along with Mr. Kneller and Mr. Spenst (men from our church in Hepburn), left before harvest started to spy out the promised land. They took up homesteads sixty miles north of St. Walburg, which was the end point of the Canadian Northern Railway. Father paid ten dollars for 160 acres of land just north of the Beaver River. He would need to have thirty acres cleared and plowed within three years in order to get a clear title for it.

He came home with stories of tall grass, miles of aspen forest, and a river full of fish, certainly a land that would flow with milk and honey given enough effort. Why, there wasn't even a rain shortage there like the rest of the province had been suffering from for the past few years.

It was harvesttime, a busy time of year even though the crops were smaller from lack of rain. We had enough hay for our own livestock, a fair crop of potatoes and onions, and some grain to sell.

"Mary, this first load of wheat goes for your tuition next year," Father promised before the trip to Hepburn with the loaded wagon.

I saw tears fill her eyes. "Oh, thank you, thank you, Father!" (Mary's dream to be a teacher someday needed money that wasn't easy to come by.)

All I could think about was our homestead. In the winter evenings, after chores and supper, Father and Rueben would sit at the table making plans. Bill joined them when he was home. (He was going to take up a homestead just east of ours.) I hung close by, not wanting to miss a word. Eaton's Catalogue didn't hold my interest this winter. I wanted to put every cent of my trap-line earnings into our homestead project.

When would be the best time to make the move? What animals would we take? How were we going to get our farming equipment there? Where would we live while waiting for a proper house to be built? How would the family be supported while brushing (clearing the land) and preparing for grain farming? These were just some of the questions that needed answers. So much was involved.

Father had bought a fine car a year earlier, but he sold it, since passable roads did not exist that far north in Saskatchewan. Uncle Jake bought our farm with the arrangement that we would continue living on it until we could move.

Finally we had it all worked out. "We'll make the move in two stages," said Father. "Bill and Rueben will help me move the heavy equipment while the muskegs and the Beaver River are still frozen. That will give us time to cut logs and build a temporary home and a barn before the rest of you arrive with the livestock and household goods. You'll need to wait till there is enough grazing for the livestock. That's when the Kneller family will be moving, so you can travel together.

"While we are gone, John and Frank will be the men of the house. I think they will manage just fine." He smiled at us.

The words men of the house had a nice ring to them, I thought. It made me feel good to think that Father had that kind of confidence in us.

The railway ran as far north as St. Walburg, so Father rented a boxcar ahead of time at Hepburn. I helped the men move the equipment—disk, plow, binder, two mowers, rake, and drill—into the boxcar. When these were all stowed inside, we fixed temporary stalls in the car for Daisy and Dolly, our big dappled Percherons, and for our saddle horses, Floss and Rock. Straw bedding on the floor helped provide surer footing for them. Tools for cutting logs and building our wilderness home, a stove for cooking and heating, rolls of quilts, and too many things to mention were all packed inside.

Mother did her part in packing provisions, including a cream-can full of her delicious zwieback—buns delicately toasted through to a pale gold. They had a slightly sweet melt-in-your-mouth quality, and they would keep forever, so long as they were dry.

Secretly, I wished I could go with the men. Their mission seemed so daring and brave. Of course, I didn't tell this to anyone. After all, Frank and Lewis were still in school, and Mother needed my help right here on the farm.

Departure morning arrived crisp, clear, and cold. It was still dark when we headed to the barn to feed and groom the horses. Yes, there was the Big Dipper, pointing north to remind us of our destination. By the time we got back to the house, the eastern sky was paling. Mother had breakfast ready. Somehow, it held no appeal for me that morning. My stomach felt strange and queasy. We took our places around the table and bowed our heads.

"Heavenly Father, bless this food . . . and may the angels protect us and bring us safely together again," Father prayed.

The men bundled up warmly. Three hundred miles in a boxcar in March was going to be a long, cold ride. Final hugs were given, and the men swung up on their horses and were off. I got to ride with them on Minnie as far as Hepburn to see them off on the train.

Several well-wishers were waiting at the train station to say good-bye. The locomotive was belching smoke and steam, bells were clanging, and men were hurrying about. Floss and Rock stamped nervously. I could tell they were not anxious to be a part of all this hubbub, but Father's and Bill's quiet manner settled them down enough to step up the ramp and into the boxcar.

The train gave a warning: "Toot, toot." Father's pleasant face appeared once more in the doorway as he reached a helping hand out to Rueben, who was clambering aboard. He then gave a final wave before the door slid shut.

I waved back and tried to call, "Cheerio!" but a huge lump filled my throat. The whistle gave a most mournful wail as the train started to move out of the station. The cars jerked and jostled, and the wheels complained on the cold rails. "Ooo-ooo!" I can still hear that lonesome whistle and feel the stinging tears that rolled down my cheeks. This new man of the house had never felt so sad and alone in all his life.

Chapter Five

Northward Bound

Surprised and embarrassed by my tears, I groped for Minnie and pulled myself onto her back. The eight-mile ride home gave me time to sort out my thoughts and feelings, and I decided that I would not disappoint Father's confidence in me.

Mother did not waste time after Father left. With her treadle machine, she sewed yards and yards of heavy canvas to cover our wagon. With some help from Uncle Jake, we boys loaded the big hayrack onto our wagon. Then we stretched the canvas cover over it, using the rack for the frame. It looked quite dandy. It made me think of the olden days stories of the American pioneers who moved westward in covered wagons, although ours was boxier than the old prairie schooners.

Meanwhile, we boys chopped lots of firewood to keep Mother's oven hot, for she was also baking batch after batch of buns. Then she sliced the buns in half and slowly toasted them in the oven like she had for Father's trip. We filled one cream-can after another with these treats for our move.

Then there was the packing. There was no space for furniture, but we would make our own. It was Mother's job to carefully choose which items she would need—the mantle clock, linens, curtains, photographs, our few books, and her most prized possession of all, her china dish set with its tiny blue flowers. These she carefully wrapped and stowed away in a washtub. The dish set was a gift from Father years earlier.

Old Betsy was traded off for a younger, newly freshened cow and her calf. Betsy was the cow we boys had practiced our milking skills on. She was an easy milker and rewarded us faithfully with a foaming bucket of fresh, rich milk. I sure hated to see her go. We kept Beauty, our Holstein, who was a heavy milker.

Mother selected a few chickens to start another flock on the homestead. I made crates for them and fastened these to the back of the wagon.

The weeks rolled by faster than I expected. The days were getting longer. The snow was gone, the fields greened up, and the songbirds returned. How I loved those prairie spring concerts. To celebrate spring further, we men of the house helped our little brother Clarence set up a play-farm behind the fir trees that grew along one side of our lane. Frank, Lewis, and I had kept a semi-permanent toy farm there for years. Rueben was the big brother who had patiently helped us tie string on our fences, make wooden sheep and horses, and build wagons and tractors whose wheels even turned on axles. We had spent many happy hours behind those evergreens. Now it was our turn to be the helpers.

May arrived . . . the month we had long awaited. There was enough fresh grass for food for our livestock along the way. Uncle Jake helped us get started, double-checking the harnesses, the horses' feet, and the well-greased wagon hubs. Unnecessary wear and tear on the horses and wagon could lead to delay and extra expense. The chickens were crated, the calf fastened in, and the cows tied to the back. We boys had done our work well.

Dick and Fanny restlessly shifted from one foot to the other, anxious to start. Lewis sat on Minnie. Rover thumped his tail nervously as he watched the whole procedure. I think he was wondering whether he was going or staying. Frank called him, and he bounded to my brother and stuck like a burr.

Mother sat on a bench in the wagon with Clarence on one side and little Don on the other. Don had two precious kittens in a basket at his feet. For now, I was the team driver, although Frank, Lewis, and I would rotate. With a couple clicks of my tongue, the two horses pulled into their collars, the wheels began to turn, and we started down the lane amid a concert of birds. Mother glanced back and waved goodbye to Uncle Jake. There sat her home of ten years, her well-worked garden and budding lilacs and maples. I saw her brush a tear away. It suddenly dawned on me that she was leaving behind her comfortable home, her relatives, and her security for . . . what? I guessed us.

Our new life on the homestead was beckoning us to hurry—360 miles to go. We joined the Kneller family near Hepburn. They had quite a caravan—fifteen cows, forty hens in crates under their wagon rack, two mules pulling a loaded democrat van (a light high wagon with a high-walled box) that we Goertzen boys took turns driving, and a covered democrat wagon that carried Mrs. Kneller and the five children. A team of big workhorses pulled this wagon, which Mr. Kneller

Northward Bound

drove. Except for Dan, the Kneller children were too young to help herd their cows, so helping Dan herd cattle fell to our lot as well. It took two of us to keep those cows moving in the right direction. To get a head start of the caravan, the herders set out while the others broke camp. You might guess that we did not cover a lot of miles each day, sometimes only ten; on a good day, maybe twenty.

Setting up and breaking down camp each day was no picnic. We tried to stop where there was water and plenty of grazing for the animals. We boys also greased the hub of every wheel each day. At each location we had to set up a stove, gather firewood, fetch water, prepare the evening meal, let the chickens run and scavenge, and hobble the horses. By nightfall, I was quite ready to sleep anywhere—comfort was not a high priority.

We traveled mostly south and a little west till we reached the North Saskatchewan River near Langham. The river was wide, and at this time of year, it ran very swift and muddy. Our crossing depended on a ferry attached to a cable spanning the river. It was a simple barge with a couple rails on the sides attached to the cable with ropes and pulleys. The operator angled the barge into the current by adjusting the length of the ropes, and the current carried it across. I was quite intrigued, watching the way it worked as we waited our turn. The raft looked a poor match for that big river. It took several trips to carry us all across. When the ferryman motioned for us to board, I took a deep breath and flicked the reins. My team paused nervously when their feet hit the hollow-sounding ramp. I gently flicked the reins again.

"Easy does it," I said reassuringly and clucked my tongue to the team.

I saw the muscles in their flanks tense as they pushed into their collars. As man of the house, I knew that I could never say whoa in a bad place. I felt my own tension drain away as we started to glide across the swollen river.

The teams had their work cut out for them on the other side of the river, for steep hills replaced the flat prairie land. Dick and Fanny took the lead. They had to stop to catch their wind. Dick usually recovered first and strained ahead until the wagon started to move, then Fanny started pulling, and the caravan would crawl on. I was as glad as they were to leave those hills behind. Now we headed northwest toward the Battlefords.

On Friday, as our caravan neared North Battleford, we spotted the boarding school that Mary attended. It was up on a hill just a few miles out of our way. Time to pitch camp for Sabbath. I dug into the work with amazing enthusiasm. I needed to set the stage for a special request. We were so close to Mary. Perhaps I could get permission for Frank and me to ride Minnie those few miles to see her.

The chores were all done and the camp looked ship-shape. Now was the time. "Mother, could Frank and I spend the day with Mary tomorrow? It's not too far. Wouldn't it be fun to surprise her?"

Mother agreed. "That does sound like fun. You may leave right after chores and breakfast."

We were pleased! We got an early start and reached the hilltop mid-morning. As we stood near the chapel, wondering what to do next, a group of girls approached. Suddenly, we heard Mary squeal, "Boys!" The next thing we knew, we were in a big bear squeeze. She introduced us to her roommate and friends, and after the church service, she took us to the dining hall for dinner before showing us around the school. But the thought of Mother and the younger boys being so close was too tempting. Her boyfriend had a car, and she asked him to drive her out to see them.

He agreed to take Mary and Frank out the next morning. I rode

Minnie back, taking a route that I thought would intercept the caravan if it left without me. I got all the way back to the campsite to find not a soul there. But how could I have missed them? What alternate route could they have taken?

I rode and rode, circled and rode some more. But they had vanished. Mr. Kneller had taken some side road, maybe to avoid Sunday traffic, but more likely, I thought, to teach those Goertzen boys not to be so frivolous.

The sun was getting low. I didn't have a blanket or even a match to light a fire. Nights were very chilly. Well, never say whoa in a bad place. I swung Minnie back toward North Battleford. By the time I reached the school campus, it was dark and late, and the campus gate was locked. I would just have to spend the night under a streetlight.

As the night wore on, I finally got so cold I mustered up the courage to approach a house and knock on the door. "I've lost my caravan and am very cold," I said to the surprised, sleepy owner. "Could I have a place for the night?" I tried to keep my teeth from chattering.

He called his wife, and she fixed a bed for me on the couch while I tethered Minnie by their garage. Did that bed ever feel good!

In the morning, the man called the police, who was able to tell him where our group was camped. My host drove me there to show me the way, and then charged my mother five dollars for my keep. It was her last five dollars. Then I had to go back to town with him to get Minnie. It was a humiliating experience for a man of the house.

During the second week of our trip, Frank and I celebrated our thirteenth birthday. It was memorable in two ways: The only water we could find to camp by was bitter, and one of the Knellers' chickens refused to come to her roost, and Rover got a little over-involved in her round-up. Like all good pioneer women, Mrs. Kneller made the best of a bad situation, which meant a big pot of chicken noodle soup, enough for both families. Problem was, the water was even too bitter for soup. We did our best to eat it.

Another weekend came. We stopped and camped at Jackfish Lake. We held our own little Sabbath School, just with our two families. I thought that was how we ought to worship more often. Singing and praying in the big outdoors, with nothing but the sky overhead, helped me know where I belonged in the scheme of things.

After that there was a leisurely time for lunch. Then came the best part, when the grown-ups and little ones napped, we boys had time to poke around and explore. There was a creek running into the lake with hundreds of tiny, one-and-a-half to two-inch fish swimming in the current. We didn't have a net to catch them, and anyway, the fish would have swum right through its holes.

"What we need is a sieve," I said. "Someone find a can while I get a hammer and nail."

Someone found an empty can, and we punched holes all over the bottom. Then Frank nailed a stick on for a handle, and we were in business. The fish swam right into the can, and we periodically dumped them into a bucket. When the bucket was about half full of these fingerlings, we figured that would do us for supper. But when we started cleaning them, we realized what a job we'd gotten ourselves into.

"Let's just chop off their heads," Lewis suggested.

You can't imagine how many heads there were, so we chose a third option—dump them into the frying pan as is. They kind of just flipped over when one side was done, to fry on the other side. (Freshly caught fish will actually sometimes flip while frying, maybe like a chicken running after its head is cut off.)

I ran to fetch some salt to make them tastier, but oops, the fish tasted sweet! My salt turned out to be sugar. Oh, well, when you're camping, it's better not to be fussy, so we ate them anyway. Actually, they didn't taste too bad, or else we were pretty hungry. Even Mr. Kneller said they were OK.

Poor Mrs. Kneller had enough worry with her own brood, but we Goertzen boys caused her a few more gray hairs, I'm sure. One day we found some old shotgun bullets in the prairie foam (the tall dry grass left from the previous summer). Now, this could provide a little fun, and I'm ashamed to admit that I couldn't help think of excitable little Mrs. Kneller. Dan was in on it too. We emptied out the buckshot and stuck it in our pockets.

That evening, we helped set up the stove as usual, set in the kindling and wood, and placed the buckshot back a ways where it wouldn't heat up too fast. Then off we went to do our chores.

I kind of watched the cooking area out of the corner of my eye. Mother came by and gave the pot a few stirs. I held my breath till she left.

After a bit, Mrs. Kneller stopped by to stir the stew, when all of a sudden . . . BANG! BANG, BANG!

"Daniel, vas ist? Vas ist?" (What is it?) she cried in Plauttdeutsch.

Mother and we boys came running. Somehow, Mrs. Kneller failed to see the humor in the situation, and poor Dan got a licking.

"Why don't you discipline your boys more?" she complained to Mother.

With a serious face, Mother replied, "Too much work!"

After a heavy spring shower one day, the wind blew away the clouds and the sun shone warmly again. It felt so good just to be alive. I felt like kicking up my heels. It must have been catchy, for all five brothers, plus the two older Kneller children, Dan and Rueben, pulled off our boots and socks and splashed and shouted through the mud puddles like a bunch of carefree puppies.

"They have to have a little fun," I heard Mother say to Mrs. Kneller.

Am I ever lucky to have a mother like her, I thought.

What excitement when we finally reached St. Walburg—360 miles in three weeks. Three cheers! In just a few days, we should reach our new home. Fortunately, we had no idea what lay ahead.

Chapter Six

Almost Home

I whistled as I busied myself with morning chores of breaking camp, and my step felt light. Hopefully, in three or four days our family would be reunited. I could hardly wait for Father to be the man of the house again, although it was with some pride that I reviewed the past couple of months, and particularly, the last three weeks. I'm glad I didn't know what awaited us. None of us could have imagined that the longest, hardest two weeks of the trip still lay ahead.

It was harder to pasture our animals this far north. The frost had just left the ground, and there wasn't much fresh grass yet. The sky clouded over and started to drizzle, but we gallantly pushed on north. The road got muddier and more slippery by the mile, and now the rain really came down. It took us days just to get to Loon Lake, about thirty miles. Well, that left only thirty miles to go. We were cold, wet, hungry, and tired as we passed the few buildings that made up Loon Lake and viewed in dismay what had become of our road. It really was an old Indian trail, never intended for teams and wagons. Rain came down by the bucketful. Muskeg swamps and brush lined the trail, which was mud, mud, and more mud. Every night, we slept in a different mud hole, stuck! We fell asleep to the whine of mosquito hordes.

Even a cow got stuck in the mud. Now, what was the right way to get a cow unstuck? I didn't know, but I had to do something, for the more she struggled, the deeper she got sucked in. Was there no bottom to the mud? It was scary to watch her. What were our resources to pull her out? Somehow, the horses were able to maneuver through the mire easier, so we used Minnie and a sturdy rope. We tied one end of the rope to Minnie's tail, the other end around the cow's horns. Minnie pulled and pulled till slurp, out came the cow. (We repeated the process again later with another cow in distress.)

Our food supplies had run out, except for Mother's zwieback, some staples such as flour, oats, and sugar, and our seed potatoes. While herding the cows along, we boys kept our eyes open for any food we could round up. It was too early for plants and berries, but we found an occasional prairie chicken or grouse. Mother would make a soup with it to serve with rationed zwieback. The Lord always provided us with something before the end of the day. When the zwieback gave out, Mother made simple pancakes with milk and flour—eggs were a thing of the past, as our few hens were on strike. I guess they were missing their old home, and all this rain was not to their liking. At least the cows were still milking.

The cows and horses didn't care for the tough, dry marsh grass left from the year before, but they had a choice of that or nothing. Swamp grass would do.

Most of our time was spent getting out of mud holes. The amazing thing was that the road continued to get worse, even when we thought it couldn't. It twisted and turned, becoming more and more narrow. Stumps and roots added challenges and variety between the mud holes. Whatever had made me think that we could be the men of the house? Getting the wagons unstuck was a lot more work than getting cows unstuck. If it hadn't been for Mr. Kneller, I don't know what we'd have done. We had to unhitch the other team from their wagon, bring them around through the mud, and hitch them to the crippled wagon. Then all four of those heavy workers would pull and strain, while we shouted encouragement and tried to find rocks or branches to give some footing for the wheels. Often, the same procedure had to be done for all three vehicles in our caravan. Sometimes it took us the better part of a day to get us all through one hole.

A very important principle was reinforced for life through these mud hole experiences—never say whoa in a bad place.

Finally, stuck in another mud hole that seemed impossible to escape from, Mrs. Kneller decided that she had had enough. "If you are too stubborn to give up this crazy homestead idea, you can do it without me," she told Mr. Kneller.

She meant it. She got her basket of eggs and set off back down the muddy trail, looking smaller than ever. We stood there, dumbfounded. But, she was one spunky lady!

Suddenly, Mr. Kneller kicked into gear and gave chase. He caught up, and they stopped near a log and talked a long while. We all breathed a sigh of relief when they got up and headed our way.

When they reached us, Mother said, "Someone needs to go for Father. It can't be too much farther."

Wonderful idea! It was quickly decided that Mr. Kneller and I would ride ahead for help. We got to the Beaver River, but the muddy torrent didn't allow us a crossing. We had no choice but to detour along the bank, through brush and swamps like you couldn't believe. We almost lost our horses in one or two of them. Six miles downstream we found a partially built bridge. We tied up our horses and picked our way across on foot.

Our homestead was only about a mile beyond that bridge. We found a small, low log cabin with a thick sod roof right close to the trail less than a mile from the top of the hill. We called, and Father appeared. Was he glad to see us, but probably not as glad as I was to see him! We told him our tale of woe, and he immediately headed back with us. What a relief to have Father shoulder the responsibility of those last few miles.

The first thing he said was, "We'll have to tear down the big racks on the wagons and leave the furniture and less necessary cargo behind for another time. The trail gets worse ahead."

And that's just what we did. In a few hours, we were off again, threading and jolting our way through the trees on a trail so narrow that the single trees and axles on the wagons rubbed and wore off the bark on the poplars alongside us. It was so rough that Mother was afraid her tub of precious blue-flowered dishes would break. Father stopped and got the tub. She had him put it on the floor between her legs, where she could keep it from tipping or bouncing. Faithful Fanny and Dick tugged the wagon around another corner. The two left wheels sank into a mud hole just as the right wheels slid on a root while climbing over a stump, almost tipping the wagon.

The unthinkable happened. Over went Mother, tub and all! I never saw so many little pieces of glass in my life. I wouldn't be surprised if you might still find some glass pieces with little blue flowers around there. Hardly a whole plate, cup, or bowl was left. Poor Mother just sat there in the mud and cried.

Darkness caught us before we could reach the river. Another night in the mud, trees, and rain, but what a difference—Father was there.

We finally reached the place where we were to cross the Beaver River, about five miles upstream from the unfinished bridge. Rueben was waiting with our other team, Daisy and Dolly, on the opposite side of the swollen river.

There was a long cable at least twice the width of the river, which at this time of year was more than 250 feet across. We unloaded a wagon and hooked the cable to it. Then Rueben's team dragged it across, rolling over and over in the current. After it reached shore, was righted and disconnected, the team on our side pulled the cable back, and we repeated the whole procedure with the next wagon, until all three were across.

Next, we herded the cows and horses down to the water. They did not like the look or sound of that swirling, muddy stream. I'm sure to them it was like jumping from the proverbial frying pan into the fire. We had to keep crowding them in until they couldn't touch bottom and were forced to start swimming. Their eyes opened wide and rolled in fright as they struck off for the far shore where they could see Daisy and Dolly. Only their heads were visible as the current carried them downstream. But they all made it.

Next, we trussed up the calves. We loaded them, the chickens, and the rest of our goods onto a raft that was left there for anyone to use. Rueben's team pulled it across.

Finally, it was our turn. We crossed on a boat that was there for public use. It took several trips back and forth to get both families across. The horses were already enjoying a feed of the good Beaver River grass.

Never Say Whoa In A Bad Place

It had taken two busy days just to make the river crossing. The last five miles to our homestead were a piece of cake. So began our life in Flat Valley.

Chapter Seven

Getting Started

Tired but triumphant, our troop arrived at our homestead cabin late that evening. But was I dreaming? I could smell the tantalizing aroma of fresh-baked bread and potato soup. Mother greeted her family and guests at the door.

So this was why Father sent Mother home with Rueben the night before. She had not wasted time. White curtains hung over the two small windows, announcing to her world that this crude log cabin was now home—and it remained home for three years before her house of lumber was finally built.

That bread and soup was the best food I had tasted in a long time. The Knellers gratefully accepted the invitation to spend the night, and beds were made up pretty well wall-to-wall—seven Knellers and eight of us in two small rooms. Interspersed here and there between the beds were cans and buckets to catch the drips from our leaky sod roof.

"I hope you don't mind," apologized Father, "but when it rains for more than five days, our roof leaks. This marsh-grass sod is not as solid as the prairie sod"

It sure beat sleeping out in a mud hole, I figured, and nobody else was about to complain.

Over the next month, it continued to rain almost daily. Father got us to help him add another layer of sod to the roof, but the rain just found new places to drip through.

Simple as our home was, passers-by were always welcomed in to share a meal or even stay the night. No one worried about lack of beds or privacy. I was surprised how many settlers were coming to this out-of-the-way place. Many came from Germany in response to a well-written ad in their newspapers by a missionary-minded priest, Father Schultz. His dream was to make this a German-Catholic district, and he was a busy man tending his flock. When I met him on the road, he called out, "Catholic or Protestant?" Since my answer was, "Protestant," that ended the conversation.

Actually, we were better off than many of the settlers—our outhouse even had a door on it! Seriously, though, Father had chosen our site wisely. It was high enough off the river to avoid flooding, yet handy to haul water for the home and the livestock. We set several barrels and cream cans on the stoneboat, a low sturdy platform built on skids and pulled by horses. (They were also used for moving rocks and roots when clearing land.) The bridge-to-be would cross the Beaver River just a mile below our place, and the trail passed close by our cabin. The river also supplied pickerel and jackfish to supplement our simple diet, and a place to take a dip on a warm day. We could float

Getting Started

logs down it for construction, and in winter it became the highway—much preferred to the summer trail. But that wasn't our homestead's only advantage.

"Look at this nice meadow," Father told the family, sweeping his arm north and westward. "It gives us a good head start on the thirty acres that needs to be cleared and broken within three years. And look, Mother, your garden can be right up here close to the house."

We worked first on breaking ground for Mother's garden, whenever weather permitted. She put in her seed potatoes, rhubarb roots, and seeds. Perhaps it was just too cool and wet, but that first year, the potatoes did very poorly. But we got a bumper crop of turnips. Turnips were not my favorite vegetable, and by the end of that first winter, I was sure I had had enough to last me a lifetime. But, again, we were fortunate. Some settlers who had planted only potatoes barely survived.

Meanwhile, we boys were kept busy that first summer working peat and manure into the soil of our meadow. We did not have much manure to work with, but the bogs were full of peat moss. It was heavy, messy work shoveling out that peat and spreading it over the field, but Father assured us it would be well worth it when we'd harvest our crop of oats next year. He figured we could clear out trees and brush in winter.

That August, as Frank and I were scouting for wild hay that we could cut for our livestock for winter, I noticed a lot of very short, small-leafed bushes with fat, dark berries on them.

"Let's check this out," I said, sliding off Minnie's back. I picked a few and popped them in my mouth. "Mmmm, delicious!"

We stopped to fill our empty lunch pail and our stomachs before carrying on our search for hay. We could hardly wait to get home with our mystery prize.

"Look what we found!" we announced to Mother as soon as we got home, popping the lid off our syrup pail.

Mother's eyes lit up. "Blueberries! We shall have pie for supper."

Talk about a treat! For several days, my brothers and I went blueberry picking. We found high-bush and low-bush blueberries, and all that rain had produced a bountiful crop of those juicy morsels. Mother canned and canned.

Later that summer, we found bright red, flat-stoned cranberries—a high-bush swamp variety. They were very tart, and made wonderful juice and jelly. What a treat those berries were for us fruit-lovers.

By this time, the Spenst family from Hepburn had joined us. The river was no longer flooded, so they just drove their wagon across. It was a little deeper than they expected, and all their chickens that were crated under the wagon were drowned. Fortunately, Knellers had a setter to get them started again. (A setter is a hen that decides it's not going to do anything but sit on a clutch of eggs until they hatch.)

Now we had three families from our Hepburn church, and we met together Sabbath by Sabbath, usually at our home, as it was a central location. Later, the Nichol and Olson families joined us.

As more homesteaders moved into the area, it was decided our settlements should be named. Mr. Brucks suggested Flat Valley for our area, as it overlooked a wide valley to the north. Eight miles farther north, the settlement became known as Goodsoil. Now that we had names, we needed post offices. Father was chosen as Postmaster for Flat Valley. He added a small room onto the front of our cabin, which became the post office. People throughout the area called him "the friendly postmaster." He also became mail carrier for both Flat Valley and Goodsoil, and he did some freighting (brought in supplies to the small stores that opened up). These jobs brought in a small income, which was a big help.

Getting Started

I joined Father every chance I got to fetch the mail from Loon Lake, delivering it to Flat Valley and Goodsoil—a round trip of seventy-five miles, twice a week over the same road we had struggled over with our loaded wagons! I not only got to spend time with Father but he often let me drive the team. This was way better than clearing brush and picking roots, but it probably wasn't very fair to Rueben and Lewis. Frank had gone to stay with Grandma and Grandpa Neufeld at Waldheim so he could continue school.

Mother's reputation had spread throughout the area, though for a reason not of her choice. She became known as the midwife, a nurse who delivers babies. One dark, chilly night in early winter there was a loud knock on our door. Father opened it to find a terrified young man. He paid no attention to Father. "Please, Mrs. Goertzen. My wife is dying. Can you come and help her? The baby can't seem to come."

"John, run hitch the horse to the sleigh," commanded Mother. Then, she hastily put string, scissors, a clean sheet, and I don't know what else into a satchel.

I slipped into my boots, coat, and hat and raced to the barn. I was soon back at the cabin, where Mother already stood waiting, all bundled up.

We followed the young man miles through the snow to a very crude, one-room cabin. The woman lay moaning on the bed. The husband was frantic. Mother asked him to go out and chop wood. She had me stoke the fire and get some hot water going, while she attended to the woman. Feeling the woman's extended stomach, she gently but firmly turned the unborn baby around inside, so that the head was pointing down. In short order there was a baby's cry, a tired but happy new mother, and a cold but relieved new father.

The story spread throughout the area, and Mother was in demand.

Never Say Whoa In A Bad Place

In vain, she protested that she was not trained. Her mother had been trained as a midwife in Europe. But Mother must have assisted her with many births, because she had a very nice way of turning the baby to make the birth easier, and she never lost a baby. If she felt things were beyond her, she was quick to send me to Loon Lake for a doctor.

There were two good doctors at Loon Lake, but usually Doctor Grady, the younger of the two, would come back with me, bringing his black bag and his guitar. When his work was finished, the baby snuggly wrapped, and his patient made as comfortable as possible, he would pull out his guitar and play and sing for the mother until she fell asleep. I thought it was so special; I will never forget it. I always liked babies, and I soon decided that birthing was one of the most special events in life. I was sure glad Mother chose me as her assistant.

In the early 1930s, a Red Cross-sponsored hospital was built in Loon Lake. On several occasions I drove a mother-to-be to the hospital. The trip was always easier in winter when we could travel by sleigh on the river.

And so our first years on the homestead flew by. I decided this was definitely the life for me. What new challenge was waiting around the next bend?

Chapter Eight

Forest Fires and Polka-Dot Pancakes

"Every able-bodied man out to fight the fires!" yelled Scotty Mitchell, the fire warden. He was recruiting firefighters, and that included me. I was fifteen that summer . . . almost grown up.

The rains of 1928 and 1929 had helped more than blueberries grow. The grass had grown outrageously tall. You might think that a rather "dry" detail, but as fall and winter came and went, that is exactly what that grass became—dry. We were still getting plenty of rain, but it came with thunder and lightening, and that thick, dry grass was like tinder. I could hardly believe how fast and furiously fire could sweep through those marshes and forests. It was one of those strange contradictions of the North that an area so wet could burn so fast. And when fire gets into peat bogs, there is almost no putting it out. There were times when, for days, I could barely see a small red ball for a sun.

On this occasion, about thirty of us were assigned to one fire. After hours of beating out flames, we had the fire contained enough so that we could take turns to hit the camp for lunch—bacon and flapjacks. Hmm, I didn't eat bacon, so that left me with flapjacks, but between having a poor cook and constant rain, those were the sorriest-looking flapjacks I ever did see.

Supper rolled around—bacon and flapjacks.

Breakfast? You guessed it, bacon and flapjacks. By this time our camp was littered with those white doughy discs, for most of the guys just ate the bacon and tossed the flapjacks.

Fortunately, with the help of the rain, we had that fire out in a couple of days. Unfortunately, Mr. Mitchell must have had a lot of fires to check on. We huddled around the smoky campfire and waited for him in the rain. None of us wanted to be fined or jailed as deserters, so we hung in there. And all I had to eat were those doughy flapjacks.

Six days later Mr. Mitchell showed up. By that time our campsite looked like the stomping ground for a herd of albino cows, with all those white "cow pies" everywhere.

"John, would you swing around to the west side of the blaze and work on containing it?"

"Yes, sir."

We were taking orders from the straw boss on another firefighting expedition. I turned Daisy and headed toward the place he had indicated. Daisy was one of our Percherons, not a saddle horse, but sometimes our workhorses did double-duty.

Once I reached our destination, I dropped Daisy's reins, slid off

Forest Fires and Polka-Dot Pancakes

her wide back, and approaching from the side. I started beating back the flames with the shovel I carried. Even with the side breeze, the heat was intense.

Suddenly the wind shifted into my face. I was right in the path of the fire. I dropped my shovel and raced for Daisy. She barely waited for me to leap on her, and she was off. I knew there was a big marsh fairly close. Could we make it?

Daisy was no racehorse, and we were in brush. It didn't take a genius to know we had no chance. I undid her halter so it wouldn't get caught in the branches. As we reached the swamp, I jumped off, gave Daisy's rump a smart whack, and shouted, "Go for it!" Then I ran deeper into the swamp grass and water.

The fire pursued me right into the swamp, burning the green grass like stubble. I waited until it almost reached me, and then I ducked under the water. I held my breath for as long as I could, and then stood back up. Sure enough, the flames had raced right over top me, and I walked back to shore. The big question was Daisy. Had she been able to outrun the fire without me to slow her down?

A few days later, I was permitted to leave for home. I had mixed-up feelings of dread and hope. Hiking back the way I figured Daisy would have run, I watched for her charred remains.

On my way home, I passed August Perschke's homestead. "Nice looking horse you have there," I called to him while passing by their place.

The Perschkes homesteaded next to the river, and August did quite a bit of horse-trading with incoming settlers, exchanging their worn-out horses for fresh ones. But this, apparently, was something different.

"If you and Frank can ride that horse, I'll pay you each a dollar," he told me. "They warned me no one could ride her, but I figured I couldn't lose for one dollar."

"I'll certainly think about it," I said, and I did, all the rest of the way home. To my relief, when I arrived home, Daisy was waiting for me. After checking her over, I went to find Frank.

"Hey, Frank. We've got ourselves a couple bucks." I shared my idea, and my twin was game.

The following day, we rode Rock and Floss into the Perschkes' field and carefully worked the flighty critter into a swamp. Then back and forth we chased her through the muck and water. Between the two of us, we never let her stop until all the fight was drained out of her.

I hopped off my horse with a bridle and ropes and walked toward her. She watched me approach, her sides heaving.

"Steady there, girl. We don't aim to hurt you," I crooned.

I put my free hand in behind her teeth and slipped the bit in, talking quietly all the while. She flinched a little as I stroked my hand down her neck, but I continued stroking and talking. She slowly relaxed. I hopped on her back and rode out of the marsh to pick up Frank, and we rode her up to Perschkes' front door, just as easy as that.

I think our neighbor was pretty surprised how quickly we earned the two dollars, but he didn't complain. Even a three-dollar horse was a bargain.

Another time, the same neighbor lost five fine, fat heifers. I think he knew we enjoyed a challenge.

"Say, boys. If you can get my heifers back, I'll let you choose whichever one you want."

We looked at each other in a way that said, "We can do this."

"Tomorrow," I told him.

The yearlings were somewhere in the brush and swamps on the south side of the Beaver River, so we got an early start with our horses the next morning. It took a while to find them, and then the fun began.

Five wild yearlings trying to streak off through the brush was a lot more challenging than a single horse in a marsh. But we persevered and were eventually able to wear them down till they were glad to be herded to the road and taken home.

Frank chose a muley, a naturally hornless cow. She turned out to be a good choice and gave us several fine calves.

But an exciting change was developing.

Rueben had been brushing (clearing land) for our friends, the Nichols, and he had saved every penny possible.

One day he told Father, "I'm ready to try my wings. I want to lease some land down on Sundance Slough and start a ranch. It's handy enough to the Nichols' that I can build a shack in my spare time, and by winter I should have enough money to buy a small herd of Herefords."

"It sounds like you've thought this through carefully," Father told him. "That's a good area for raising hay, too. I can loan you one of our horses to get started."

His ranch was fourteen miles upriver, so we didn't see a lot of him. But after the river froze over, he dropped by to tell us he was going for the cows.

"Could the boys give me a hand?"

Things went pretty good until we got to the river. The ice was supposed to make the crossing a cinch, but we were mistaken. Those Herefords took a very dim view of ice, and do you think we could chase or coax those critters across? We thought and thought. Finally, we caught them one by one and dragged them over the ice with our saddle horses.

It was getting dark, and we still had two more cows to pull across. I said, "Boys, what do you say about me going up to the cabin and making supper for us? By the time you get there, I'll try to have a nice pile of pancakes ready for you."

Sounded good to them, so away I went. I soon had a fire going, so I went out to get some snow to melt, since Rueben didn't have a well for water. But rabbits were very plentiful, and it was hard enough to get snow without "raisins" in daylight, let alone in the dark. So instead, I decided to go down to the river, chop a hole in the ice, and get clean water. That gave me plenty of time to come up with a plan.

I mixed up a big bowl of batter, adding a handful of real raisins that I had spotted earlier in Rueben's supplies. By the time the boys came trooping in, things smelled pretty good, aside from the smoking rag stuck in a can of coal oil that was standing in for lamp duty.

"Come and sit down to eat," I invited them, setting a plate stacked high with pancakes in the middle of the homemade table.

Right after the blessing, I warned, "It was a little dark for me to see the snow very well. I tried to be careful, but you might want to keep a lookout for"—I cleared my throat—"for any rabbit droppings I might have missed."

The boys dug in without comment. The light wasn't very good, but they were obviously watching. I noticed Rueben suddenly pause, remove something from his mouth, set it to the side, and continue eating. One after the other, I saw the boys pause, remove a raisin, and bravely continue eating.

Rueben was on his third raisin before he actually bit into one. "Aw, I'm eating 'em anyway," he announced, pulling out the two from under his plate and digging in with more enthusiasm.

Before the meal was over, we all had a good laugh, as we cleaned up our caches of raisins from under our plates.

Some days later, a few of Rueben's cows turned up missing.

"Do you want me to try and find them?" I offered. I had done a

Forest Fires and Polka-Dot Pancakes

fair amount of tracking, although fresh snow was going to complicate things.

"Please, may I go with you?" begged Clarence. He was only about 8, but he was a plucky little guy, and good company. Why not let him come.

The area was too brushy for riding, so we set off on foot. The snow was fairly deep. Ah, here were hoof prints. We followed them quite a ways before I started getting suspicious.

"Let me check these prints a little better," I said to Clarence, stopping and carefully brushing the fresh snow off a track. It was too splayed for my liking.

"Oh, no," I groaned. "These are moose tracks, not Rueben's cows!"

Now what? It was getting dark, it was snowing and blowing, and we were who knows where. Clarence was bravely following my steps through the deep snow.

"Are we lost, John? Will we die in a snow bank?" he asked with a little tremble in his voice.

"Come on, Clarence," I told him. "We don't know where we are, but we are not really lost. So long as we keep going downhill, we'll hit Beaver River sometime. And so long as we keep going, we won't die in a snow bank."

"I'm so tired!" he said, but he hung in there.

We tramped through the snow all night and reached the river early the next morning. We soon found an empty cabin, and it didn't take me long to get a fire going. While we were warming up, we snooped around for some food. The only thing we found was some white sugar. We helped ourselves to a little of it before continuing on. Of course, once we hit the river, I knew we were just a few miles from Rueben's.

I don't remember the outcome of the lost cows, but I sure was thankful for the outcome of the lost boys.

That winter, I set up a successful trap line that I ran for several years. But that began a whole new set of adventures.

Chapter Nine

Trapper and Farm Hand

"It looks like another night by the fire," I spoke aloud to myself, shifting the growing pack of pelts to a more comfortable position and checking the growing blush pink in the afternoon sky.

It had been a good day on my trapline. Every snare had given me something, but each trap had to be carefully reset, and the animals skinned.

"I'll certainly have a nice little bundle of money to add to the family purse this week." Talking to myself made it seem less lonely out here in the wilderness.

Bunny trails zigzagged in every direction through the miles of brushy aspen forests. It was rabbit-heaven, and we were in a plague-year in their cycle.

The biggest bulk of my pack was rabbit and muskrat pelts.

Swamps are the environment muskrats thrive in. Muskrats are water rodents, much smaller than beavers, with a stringy rat-like tail. Their lodges are small messy-looking humps of rushes and coarse grass.

But I also caught coyotes, ermine (weasels in their white winter fur), and an occasional lynx or fox.

With such an abundance of fur-bearers, it made good sense for me to set up a trapline. Winter and early spring is when the furs are prime—thick and worth more. I also had an easier time getting around, for I had the frozen river for a highway.

I had miles of trapline that needed to be checked several times a week. I didn't want coyotes feeding on my snared rabbits. Besides, the quicker I reset the snares, the more pelts I could bring in. Often, I didn't make it home for the night. I carried a backpack for my furs and a little food—a hunk of bread and a chunk of venison. Tied on a strap was a big tin cup to melt a little snow. On a cold night even plain hot water helped keep me warm and satisfied. Sometimes one of my brothers was along. Sometimes I was alone, like now.

"Time for me to collect enough wood for the night and get a fire going."

That night as I sat alone nursing my campfire, I heard the howl of a wolf. It was not an uncommon sound, and when I was snug in bed at home, I actually thrilled to hear it—so haunting and wild. But in the dark, alone, it made my skin prickle. I sometimes ran across wolf tracks, but with dense forest and their natural fear of man, I seldom saw one. I reassured myself of this as I heard the howl again. I whittled on a stick just to help pass the time, and then I stopped to add a chunk of wood to my fire. That's when I noticed two shining eyes staring at me from the woods. I stared back. The eyes moved a little closer, stopped, then moved again.

What was behind those eyes? I couldn't see any shape in the darkness, just those lighted eyes. I thought it wise to clear my throat to alert whatever it was that I was there—perhaps it hadn't noticed me.

The eyes stopped again, and then proceeded in my direction. I reached for my shotgun, just in case. I really didn't want to use it, for it held my last bullet. Ammunition cost money, and I didn't go around wasting shots.

But my unknown visitor seemed intent on its purpose even though it knew I was there—or was it because I was there!

I couldn't stand the suspense any longer. I raised my gun. Bang! The two shining eyes were gone.

The next morning, as soon as there was enough light, I went over to check on last night's predator. To my chagrin, it was nothing but a rabbit—Yes, only a rabbit! The shotgun hadn't left much more than the skin behind.

Another night, as I sat by my fire, a mouse scurrying about in the firelight entertained me. Suddenly, I got an idea. I usually traded my furs at George Seeley's store down on Beaver River Flats. He had a sign posted that read "Will buy any fur." I would see if he held true.

I tapped the mouse smartly on the nose with a stick—animals' noses are very sensitive, something to remember if you are carrying a stick and are attacked by a dog or other animal. After killing the mouse, I carefully skinned the tiny creature by firelight. Perfect!

When I presented my mouse pelt along with my other furs, Mr. Seeley laughed and laughed until I started to squirm. But he was true to his word. He bought the tiny pelt and hung it right on his sign in his shop. He paid more for that little mouse pelt than for a rabbit. Might there be a market for mouse pelts?

"I could get you more, if you like." I tried not to sound too eager.

"No, thank you. One is just what I need," he assured me.

I was always looking for a new area to set up my trapline, so when someone told me about a lake that was thick with muskrats, it sounded like something worth checking into. I took a horse and the ever-willing Clarence to check it out. I decided the muskrats were just as plentiful and more easily available on my own line. But as we headed back, we spotted a skunk, a really big one! Now, a skunk pelt was worth a lot more than rabbit or muskrat. I had read how to do it right. I mustn't pass up a chance to try it out.

"Watch this, Clarence," I said to my admiring little brother. "I know a way to kill a skunk so it doesn't smell bad."

The whole trouble was that it didn't work. It smelled very bad! We decided we would not touch it with our hands, so we trussed up its legs and tied it to the saddle, feeling quite pleased that we managed all this without actual contact.

We got home rather late. The house was already dark and quiet, so we crept in, trying not to wake up our brothers. We had hardly shut the door, when Lewis' voice said, "Where's the skunk?"

Well, so much for odor-free skunk catching!

That spring Father gave me permission to use twenty-five dollars of my earnings to buy my very own saddle horse. Ruby was a shiny black mare. Included with her were a saddle, a bridle, a martingale (a strap that comes up between the horse's front legs with rings for the reins to pass through to steady the horse's head), and a blue felt blanket.

I felt like I was riding on cloud nine for sure. Those long miles trudging through the snow and long nights sitting by a campfire were a small price to pay for my very own horse. I was fifteen.

To make things even better, Mary came home. I hadn't seen her since that fateful weekend Frank and I visited her on our way past North Battleford two years ago. The summer before, she had sold books to earn her tuition to complete her last year of high school. How good it was to have her back. We had always enjoyed riding together, and she was duly impressed with my beautiful Ruby.

When summer rolled around, Mother, Mary, and a few of us boys made the long trip to Saskatoon for my very first camp meeting. The preaching was good, but between the meetings was the best. I hadn't really missed a social life, because I hadn't ever known one. But to have all these young people around, including some shy, pretty girls . . . well, that was something new for me. I was definitely going to try to do this again some time.

Sheila Large and her parents were especially warm to me. Sheila had been Mary's roommate at the boarding school, and she still remembered Frank and me from our visit two years earlier.

"Why don't you go back to Arlee with us?" her folks urged me. "We know a returning soldier who's looking for a farmhand for harvesting. We're sure you could get a job with him."

My ears perked up—a job was something I'd be interested in. So I became a bona fide farmhand for Jack Innis near Biggar, Saskatchewan. (The tiny town of Biggar is still there with a sign that reads, "New York is big, we are Biggar.")

Upon arriving at Jack's farm, I could see that he had a preference for roans—all twelve of his horses were either red or blue roans. He believed in pasturing the horses out overnight—all of them. So my first duty each morning was to hike out to the pasture, bring the horses into the barn, give them their grain, brush them down, and harness them.

It didn't take me long to figure that I would save a lot of time and shoe leather if I could keep one horse at the barn to ride out to the pasture. As tactfully as I knew how, I made the suggestion to my employer, who was definitely a stern military figure in my eyes.

He looked me up and down and asked, "What's wrong with your legs?"

That ended that idea.

I worked hard the rest of the summer and right through harvest before heading home via Saskatoon and our old stomping grounds. Martha Brucks met me there. My brother Bill had married her pretty, dark-haired sister Hilda, and when they heard that I was coming home, they had gotten in touch with Martha.

"I'd like to go visit my sister. I'll pay for your train ticket to St. Walburg if I can travel with you," Martha told me.

What a deal! The Bruckses had been our neighbors at Carson, and I loved the idea of traveling with Martha for company. She packed a nice lunch of roasted chicken and bread, and we had a wonderful trip.

From St. Walburg I caught us a ride on a truck all the way to Loon Lake. There I found a friend that was happy to have us join him the rest of the way by wagon.

We were passing the last homestead before ours. The large family lived in a poorer than average shack close to the road. The children were rather unkempt but very friendly. As usual, they came tumbling out of the house to wave and see who was passing by. It was already late enough in the fall that the ground was frozen, but they were all barefoot. The oldest girl's feet suddenly slipped out from under her on the icy slop heap. Down she went, her skirt flying up over her head.

Martha was quite mortified at this introduction to frontier life.

Soon after we arrived home, and I handed Father my hard-earned summer's wages—thirty-five dollars.

Chapter Ten

Riding the Rails

"I'll go get Frank. I'll ride the rails. Lots of guys are riding the rails these days, so why not me?"

Father looked at me in shock, but this wasn't just a thoughtless outburst. I had been thinking about it for a while, so when Father voiced his worry about the lack of money to send a ticket for Frank to come home, I was ready to volunteer.

Frank was really serious about getting an education. The first two years after our move up north he boarded with relatives in Waldheim for the school term, close to where we lived at Carson. Then the Gardners, visiting from Assiniboine, Manitoba, offered him an education in return for his help on their farm.

Riding the Rails

We were now experiencing the Great Depression. Almost everyone was hard up. The farmers' crops were failing because of no rain. Their rich black soil blew away in the wind, making dust blizzards. Men and boys flocked to the city to try to find jobs, but there just weren't enough jobs to go around. It was a very difficult time.

In Flat Valley, we certainly did not lack for rain, but money was a different story. The school year was over, and Father wanted Frank home, but money was not to be found.

"I'll go get him," I said again.

"It's not as easy as it might sound," Father warned. "Although those trains don't move fast, you've got to know when to get on and jump off. You'll be rubbing shoulders with all sorts of unsavory characters. And I hear the railway companies are getting real rough on hobos they catch. Besides, do you have any idea of the distance we're talking about?"

We discussed it further, but in the end, he gave his permission. I hugged Mother and promised her that Frank would be home in a few weeks.

A few days later, I caught a ride to St. Walburg. That far north there wasn't much worry about hobos—there just weren't enough people of any sort. I was able to stow away without a hitch.

At the Battleford station, I hid in the coal bin of a freight train and waited for it to start. The conductor made his way along the long wooden platform, checking for stowaways. I had my eye up to a knothole, watching his progress.

He stopped at the coal bin and looked directly at my knothole—it was like our eyes locked. My heart stood still!

But he turned and continued his inspection. I'll never know if he actually saw my eye in that knothole or not, but I sure was relieved to hear the toot of the whistle and feel the train pull out of the station.

Never Say Whoa In A Bad Place

A few miles out of Langham, as the train began to slow down, I hopped off to avoid a bigger train station. Several other guys did the same. Word was out that the railroad inspectors here could get real rough with railroad bums.

I started hiking toward Hepburn. It was a long ways to Assiniboia, Manitoba, but maybe I could just hitch hike the rest of the way. (Hitch-hiking was a whole lot safer in those days than now, as was riding trains.)

It was a beautiful morning. The sun felt so warm and good, and I was so tired. Why not just stretch out on that little knoll for a bit . . . Next thing I knew, I heard a horn honking.

I sat up, and there was a nice sedan. A pleasant-faced fellow called, "Would you like a ride this way?"

Would I! As I hopped in, he told me he would take me to the next town, and then he handed me three whole chocolate bars. He was a salesman, he told me. "When you buy a bar, remember, you want Neilson's Jersey Milk."

He must have been a good salesman, because I still remember what he said.

We got to the next little town, and he kept on going. "I just said that so I could drop you off if I didn't like your company. You've got a ride to Winnipeg if you want it."

Talk about a trip in luxury! My mother was praying for me, I know.

I connected up with Frank at our brother Herb's place, and we set off for home, riding the freights without incident. A few miles out of Regina, we jumped off to avoid being picked off. (Remember, trains traveled a lot slower then.)

We hiked along the tracks. I felt a little smug at how adept we were getting at this, when Frank said, "Do I hear footsteps catching up to us?"

We listened as we kept walking. Yes, those steps were definitely gaining on us. We stepped up our pace. Our pursuer did the same. We were tempted to run for it, but where to? And besides, that would look suspicious.

A man in uniform caught up to us, asked us a few questions, and then out of the clear blue, asked, "Are you boys hungry?"

"Well . . . yes," we answered cautiously.

"I work here as a rail inspector, and I'm just on my way in for supper. I'd like you to join me."

Frank and I exchanged glances, not sure what he was up to. But what choice did we have? We went along.

He took us to a restaurant, ordered a nice supper for himself, and encouraged us to order whatever we wished! We both ordered a modest but pleasant meal of beef stew, and then we asked the nice man for his name and address so we could repay him.

He wouldn't hear of it. He told us of how years earlier, he and four friends were hunting for jobs without any luck. They were discouraged and hungry, not knowing what to do next. A gentleman came along and insisted on buying them all a good supper. For payback, he asked them to pass it on someday. Seeing us boys, he suddenly remembered he had never fulfilled his end of the bargain.

At the Regina station, Frank and I split. Frank continued on home, but I turned and headed back toward Manitoba. A plan had been growing in my mind to return to my brother Herb. I might be able to get some work and help things out at home.

I checked an eastbound freighter and found a carload of ties of various lengths . . . not a bad place to spend the night. It was already dark. I wedged in between some ties and settled down for the wait.

Never Say Whoa In A Bad Place

I could see the swinging light from a lantern. It must be from the conductor on the platform checking the cars for stowaways. This was the test. I pulled my Salvation Army coat a little tighter around me and hugged the ties, turning my face away as the lantern-bearer approached. His footsteps stopped. I held my breath. Finally, I turned my head to see what he was doing. He was shining his light right on me!

"Come on out of there," he said sternly. "And don't even think of jumping off the other side."

What a wonderful idea! Almost before the words were out of his mouth, I shot out the other side and ran along the track. Even as I ran, the train jerked and started to move. As it gained on me, I kept running until my car reached me. I grabbed onto a tie, swung up, and scrambled back into my original hiding place, where I spent the night.

The next morning, while stopped at a small station, fellow travelers shared stories of the rough treatment for bums from here to Winnipeg. I decided it was again time to change my mode of travel.

I hiked, caught rides, and worked for meals. Usually, I chopped wood for a housewife in exchange for a bowl of soup. One evening I was ready for a change of pace.

I stopped at a Chinese restaurant and asked if I could wash dishes to earn a meal.

The owner said, "Yes, yes, but no wash dishes. Come."

He took me to the back where the cooks were all busy and pointed up to the water pipes high overhead. They were black with smoke and grease and covered with spider webs. He set up a tall ladder, propping the bottom against a table stacked high with dirty dishes.

I eyed the set-up warily and suggested we nail down a board to keep the ladder from slipping.

"No, no slip," he assured me, pointing to the heavy table.

So up I went and set to work.

I was almost finished—one pipe to go. I tried to reach a little farther, when my ladder started to slide down the wall—bump, bump, bump, faster and faster down the wall, till CRASH! The table tipped, and I landed in a heap of broken dishes.

The little man came rushing over. He was so relieved to find me unhurt, he wouldn't even hear of me finishing my job. He gave me the best meal I had in a very long time; in fact, it lasted me another couple of days—all the way to Winnipeg.

From Winnipeg, I had only one leg of my journey left. With my last fifteen cents, I bought a chunk of beef bologna and a loaf of bread. Black from soot and dirt, I headed toward Maple Ridge where Herb lived, contentedly munching on my bread and bologna.

A car appeared ahead, slowed down, and stopped beside me. Herbert sat behind the wheel, a big grin on his face. "I told my friend 'way back there that there was something familiar about that fellow's walk. Would you like to join us back to Winnipeg?"

I settled into the back of his Model A among the crated eggs.

The Joke's on Me

Herbert told me I had come to the right place if I wanted to work. The Canadian Railway was buying firewood as fast as it could be produced, at ninety cents a cord. He was taking advantage of this opportunity himself to supplement his small income from selling eggs and honey.

I borrowed one dollar and twenty-five cents from him for a Swede saw blade, and I was ready to go. We camped in the woods during the week and spent all our time cutting and piling firewood. I learned how to make good use of that long Swede saw. Soon, I was cutting three to four cords a day, and that included properly piling it. I would be well-to-do one of these days if I could keep this up.

Never Say Whoa In A Bad Place

Out in the bush, I took my turns being cook and chief bottle washer, and as I remember it, our choice of fare was soybeans and rice, three times a day—a new diet for me. I really began to appreciate soybeans.

But it wasn't all work and no play. We had some cousins from the Frank Goertzen family living only about 40 miles east of Herb's, at Steinbach. Herb decided to pay them a visit, and I was more than happy to go along.

I was staying with Carl and his widowed sister, Elizabeth. Next door was the Geisbrecht family, with five girls and one boy. Dietrich, the boy, was fourteen. His sisters were all older, up to age twenty-two. I had gotten acquainted with them, and discovered that the girls were fun to tease, so long as I minded my p's and q's.

I learned that their parents were going to be gone for the day, and I suddenly got hit with a streak of mischief. I borrowed Carl's big overalls, rubbed black soot all over my face and hands, pulled a cap over my head, and headed next door for a visit.

I knocked, and Dietrich answered. A look of surprise and fear crossed his face. I said very politely in English, "Could I have something to eat and a bed for the night?"

"No, no. Try the bachelor over there," and he pointed to Carl's place next door.

I lowered my voice and said in Low German, "I'm John . . ."

Just then, one of the girls called out the window in Low German, "I take pity on that poor fellow. I'm going to the pump house to get some cold milk for him." Then she quickly added, "But don't let him in the house. Keep him in the summer kitchen." (A summer kitchen was kind of an open room built near the kitchen door, where the ladies would do their cooking, baking, and canning when it was hot in an effort to help keep the house cool.)

Riding the Rails

While she ran to fetch the milk, another girl ran to get some zwieback and butter. Suddenly, I heard horse hoofs and wagon wheels. Oh, no. Mr. Geisbrecht was a very serious man, and I was caught. Before Dietrich ran out to take the horses, I told him, "Tell your folks who I am." But by the time he got out there, his mother had come around to the house, so he only told his father.

Meanwhile, the girls were telling their mother all about this poor black man. It was interesting to sit there listening, when they never guessed I understood every word they said.

"Oh, yes, girls, if anyone asks for food, it is our duty to feed him." She sent them scurrying, while she herself put a chair on the shady porch for me.

I quietly told her, "I'm John."

Her hand flew to her chest. "Och, Mein Gott!" was all she said.

Mr. Geisbrecht came to the porch. "Come in, come in," and he pointed me toward the door.

I furtively slipped into a chair just inside the door. But even behind his whiskers, he could not hold back a chuckle.

"What are you laughing at, Father? This is not funny! That guy, we don't want him in the house," said the oldest sister.

I gave her a sideways look.

"Martha, we'll get the bed ready for him in your room," Mr. Geisbrecht said brightly.

"Oh, no, Father! He's not sleeping in my room."

Everything was uncomfortably quiet for a moment, when one of the girls blurted, "It looks to me like he just painted himself."

Time to go! I shot out the door, but not before one of the girls grabbed me by the shirt, popping several buttons. All five girls were in hot pursuit, and I ran, over the fence, through the garden, past Carl's house, and into his barn. They were sturdy farm girls, and they were out to get even with me for being humiliated.

I scrambled up into the hayloft, swung myself out the window onto the ledge, and pulled myself onto the roof. Whew! I was out of reach—at least for the moment—for as they left, they warned, "We'll get you yet!" I figured they meant it.

I persuaded Herb that we really needed to get an early start back to Hazel Ridge the next morning.

Chapter Eleven

A Good Trade

My woodcutting fortunes ended prematurely because of a bee—a small honeybee.

Herb raised honeybees as a side business to bring in a little extra income. One day I connected with a bee the wrong way, and it stung me on the knuckle. I didn't think too much about it, but that knuckle grew huge, and instead of getting better, it got worse. Infection set in, and poultices and hot water did not help.

It was on my right hand, and there was no holding a Swede saw. I got sick with a high fever, and Herb said, "It's time to see a doctor."

I was put in the hospital where the doctor figured I'd get better in a hurry with the new wonder drug—penicillin. I think the dose may have been pretty high, but instead of helping me, I got a major allergic reaction to it. That was almost curtains closed for me.

I just couldn't seem to get back on my feet. It was obvious I would not be cutting wood for some time to come.

"I think it would be best for you to go home to recuperate, but you're NOT riding the rails," Herb told me.

"I agree. I'm not up to that, but I don't know if hitchhiking is that much easier."

Herb thought a bit. "You've got a nice little nest egg from your woodcutting. You can buy a bike. I'll take you to the big Eaton's store in Winnipeg next time I take in the eggs."

I hesitated briefly but decided I couldn't come up with anything better at the moment.

Setting off for home in grand style on my brand new bike, I ran into a stiff, cold headwind. By the time I reached Minnidosa, thirty or so miles from Winnipeg, I felt faint and sick. Surely this could not all be from a little bee sting. Maybe I was getting polio, I thought, for there was a polio epidemic in Manitoba at the time. Home seemed unreachable. What could I do?

As I was trying to think this through, I saw a fellow closing his garage. Before the door closed, I saw three used Model T Ford cars inside.

I pulled up on my bike and asked, "How'd you like to trade one of those Fords for a brand new bike?"

"Business is pretty slow. People just don't have enough money to buy gas. I think I'll take you up on that offer," said the salesman.

I had seldom ridden in a car, let alone driven one. It had no license, but neither did I. The salesman backed it out for me, put in a few gallons of gas to get me started, and I proudly drove off in my very own rig.

It was nearing nightfall, so I stopped for the night in a brushy area just a few miles out of town. I was up early the next morning, eager to use my new wheels. I gave it a few good cranks, just like the salesman had. It sputtered. Another crank, and it started right up.

My, it was gratifying to see those fence posts go by so quickly! As the sky started to lighten, I could make out a line to my right. Was it a road or a train track? I strained to see, when suddenly, bumpity-bump, my car went into the ditch, through the fence, over some furrows, through another fence and ditch, and after another big BUMP, everything was quiet and still. Somewhere along the way, my hood had flown off. My car now stood on the unknown road, facing the road I had just left, but it was dead.

Now I really felt sick. I got out, fetched the hood, and clipped it back on, wondering what to do next. If only I still had a simple bicycle. Well, I might as well give the thing a crank and see if there was any spark. Fortunately, it started right up. I climbed in and continued on my way, wiser. This critter had no eyes but my own to watch where it was going.

In Rosthurn, I stopped at Uncle Isaac's. What a happy surprise, Mother and Father were there. Father promptly bought a license for five dollars, and we drove to Loon Lake, as far as the road allowed. (I got my driver's license a year later for thirty-five cents. Some years later, I sold my Model T to Lewis.)

Chapter Twelve

Arrested

"Have you heard that the new constable is in town?" That news always brought some excitement. I was always interested to see what mount he brought. It was usually a pretty smart-looking horse. And it was an exciting day when higher officers came to inspect the new recruit and put him through his paces. In his smart Royal Canadian Mounted Police (RCMP) uniform, he would pull out a white handkerchief and brush across the horse to see if it was really clean. Then the new officer would put the horse through his maneuvers. It was quite a show that I didn't like to miss, and it seemed like we got a new constable often. From 1931 to 1937, we were served by Constables Seaman, King, Marshall, and Bingham, all fine young men.

Game wardens were also a part of northern law enforcement. I believe the first one in our area was Paul Rafuse, an outgoing, sociable fellow who rode a half-broke black Standard called Jazz. Like the other officers, he would often stop by for a friendly chat and a warm meal. When sister Mary returned home, he had even more reason to stop by. He ended up becoming my brother-in-law. Although he was a big guy with an even bigger voice, he had a soft heart for the pioneers who were struggling to stay alive. I think many times he chose not to see some of the hunting and fishing infractions.

But that was not the case with some of the more idealistic wardens. Game Warden Revel was one of these, and he conscientiously did his best to enforce the new law about licenses. He traveled by boat up and down the river to check for nets. One day he stopped by and was happy to accept an invitation to stay for dinner. While he ate, we boys high-tailed it down the river a mile to pull in the fish net and hide our catch up over the hill. Another time, he tried to track Frank Nichols deer hunting. Frank made huge circles of tracks to add a little challenge. After leaving the warden far behind, he carried the shot deer to the warden's vehicle and left it as a gift in the back seat.

As postman, Father was given a pile of hunting and fishing licenses. He was to sell these, but money was in short supply, and with some families, it was nonexistent.

"Boys," he said one day. "I hear our neighbors are pretty hard up. They're out of food. Could you give them a hand?"

We knew what he meant, so Lewis went out and got a deer. He took it to the hungry family. Deciding to take full advantage of the kind deed, the man reported to the game warden that the Goertzen boys had killed a deer. Of course, he didn't mention whom it was for. There was a fifteen-dollar reward for reporting hunting without a license, which was quite a sum in those days. He decided that he would have his meat and the reward money to boot.

The warden came to check it out.

"If there is any meat here, you'll find it in that bin," Father told him, pointing out the meat bin.

The warden hunted around. The best he could come up with was an old deer leg with no meat on it, but it would have to work as evidence. The fifteen-dollar reward had to come from somewhere.

Lewis was summoned to court. I couldn't believe this was happening to my gentle brother all because he helped a neighbor. Surely the judge would see through the whole scheme and acquit him. I went along to give Lewis some moral support.

The verdict? Guilty. He was fined fifteen dollars.

"That judge was in cahoots with the warden, I'll bet," I fumed on our way home. The idea of paying the government for the right to eat a wild animal was still a new one for me.

Father gave Lewis the money for the fine, and I rode with him to Goodsoil. We went into the police office, and the officer lit into us like we were the worst hooligans around! Lewis and I looked at each other, turned on our heels, and walked out the door. Somehow, this all seemed so wrong to us.

"I'd rather sit in jail than pay that fine!" Lewis told Father when we got home, handing him the fifteen dollars.

Father did not like the idea of a son in jail, but he told Lewis that he'd respect that choice.

Every two weeks the police came by hoping for the money. Each time he would ask, "When are you going to pay that fine?" I don't think he wanted to make an arrest. What he needed was the money.

Finally, on his fourth visit, he took Lewis into custody and drove him to St. Walburg, almost seventy miles from Goodsoil. From there, Lewis was to be sent by train to Mooseman. Since he was under age, the officer had to accompany him. The officer wired ahead to say he was bringing in a juvenile.

They asked him, "For what crime was he charged?"

"For shooting a deer without a license."

"Take him back home. We don't have room for that kind," was the reply.

Now what? The embarrassed officer had to save face about the jail sentence, so he took Lewis back to the police barracks in Goodsoil and kept him in custody for seven days. He spent the night in a cell. Each meal at the boarding place cost the officer thirty-five cents. He certainly came out on the short end of the stick on that one. But there didn't seem to be any hard feelings, for he continued to stop at our place for a meal and a chat. (Maybe it helped recoup all those thirty-five cent meals he paid for.)

Chapter Thirteen

Unexpected Company

I held the reins loosely as the wagon jostled and bounced along the trail toward Loon Lake. Clarence was telling me about his teacher, Miss Lange. I was sure glad a school had opened in Flat Valley. The first few years Clarence had gone with Frank back to Waldheim and stayed with our grandparents, but he was so young. It was hard for him to be so far from home.

Suddenly my thoughts were interrupted.

"Did you see that flash?" I asked Clarence. "That looked like a reflection off of glass."

It had been raining till just a bit ago, but the sun had broken through the clouds. What could be through those trees to catch the

Unexpected Company

light like that? Surely not a vehicle!

Our wagon rounded the next corner, and sure enough, there was a high four-door Essex sedan stuck in a mud hole. Even more surprising, beside it were Uncle Henry Feyerabend and Grandfather Neufeld surveying the situation. Inside the car sat Aunt Annie, my cousins, Anna Marie and Ruth, and Grandmother Neufeld.

After we shared our happy greetings, Uncle Henry said, "Am I ever glad you showed up. Would you pull me through this mud hole, and we'll be on our way?"

"I'd be glad to," I told him. "But the next ten miles are the worst. I don't think you'll make it through. Tell you what. I'll just pull you out of this hole. Then why don't you park the car and enjoy the break, and I'll pick you up tomorrow on my way back with the mail."

I unhitched Dick and Fannie and hooked them to the car. Soon, we had them out and continued on our way.

I had made this mail-and-freight run many times with Father. It was usually a two-day trip to Loon Lake and then back to Goodsoil, but it was only this summer that I had been sworn in as a bona fide mail carrier and could make the run on my own. It was a treat to have Clarence along to help wile away the hours. He was a good talker and listener.

I glanced down at Clarence. "Seeing Grandmother reminds me of a story. Once upon a time long ago," I began, "Grandmother came to visit us."

"Like now?" Clarence interrupted.

"Sort of," I said, "except that she brought her special black satchel. For some reason, Father bundled Frank and me and Lewis up and took us to the neighbors' for the night. When we came back the next morning, you'd never guess what was in the parlor—a basket. And in the basket was a baby all bundled up. Our big tabby cat was lying against the basket purring very loudly. Little Lewis said, 'I bet kitty thinks it's a tiger.' But it was YOU."

"Tell me another one, a longer one this time," begged Clarence.

And so the miles went by. At Loon Lake we loaded the freight first thing in the morning, picked up the mail, and headed back up the trail, looking forward to picking up our visitors.

I guess Uncle Henry hadn't quite gotten the picture. The next day we found them hopelessly stuck in another mud hole. They seemed quite ready to settle down on some sacks of mail and ride home with me through the ruts and mud.

Mother was so happy to see her parents and sister that she cried. They were in a sense our first true visitors in Flat Valley—people who had traveled specifically to see us. And to make it even better, we were now in our new house.

On our way out to do chores the next morning, we invited Anna Marie and Ruth to come to the barn and see the animals. The girls enjoyed the kittens, and even the calf was cute, but the way Anna Marie wrinkled up her nose, I could tell they were distinctly uncomfortable with some of the other aspects of barn life.

I put some fresh hay in the manger for the cow and pulled up a little stool to milk her, tucking the milk bucket between my knees. Soon, the bucket was full of foaming milk.

"Watch this," I said to the girls. I set the bucket aside and immediately the mother cat approached me, purring loudly. I shot a stream of milk her way, and she caught it in her mouth. You could tell this was no trial run for her. I offered for the girls to try it, but no sirree!

At the breakfast table a bit later, do you think those girls would put any milk on their porridge or in their glasses? "Only bottle milk for us!" I tried to keep a straight face. I wonder where they thought bottled milk came from.

Unexpected Company

Uncle Henry was a real sportsman. He wore leather spats on his legs and leather cuffs, just like it showed in the Eaton's catalog. We went fishing, and he caught a three-foot jackfish. After cleaning it, he soaked it in salt water and then smoked it for two days—quite the process.

Our duck-hunting expedition was another story.

"The marshes have hundreds, maybe thousands of ducks, so success is assured," I told Uncle Henry, as our little company wound through the brush.

We quietly approached a swamp. A great blue heron lifted off, and one of the boys shot. With a whoosh and a whir, hundreds of ducks took to the air.

We sloshed on to another marsh. I carefully explained how to use the triggers and levers and how to crawl through the reeds until the water got too deep. "Then, just stand up and quickly shoot at the cloud of ducks. You can't miss with a twelve-gauge shotgun."

BANG! The gun fired—both barrels. But he hadn't raised the gun yet—and there went the second flock of ducks. No ducks for supper.

Uncle Henry was a professional candy maker. He had been making candy since he was fifteen. Why not invite all the neighbors to a candy party? We spread the news to bring a few pounds of sugar and come join the party. The neighbors came, bringing along more than one hundred pounds of sugar, and Uncle Henry started making candy. Did he make candy? Hard candies, caramels, taffy, and chocolates like we had never tasted before. After an evening of fun, people went home with bags full of candy.

Our grandparents seemed to enjoy every minute of their stay. They were in their eighties. Grandfather couldn't hear much, and Grandmother couldn't see much, so they sat side by side. Grandmother told Grandfather what was being said, and Grandfather told Grandmother what was happening.

All too soon, our happy week with them was over. I would take them back to their car the next morning. The evening before, Grandfather brought out a very old cowbell that he had brought from Europe.

"This has been hanging around my shop long enough. Would you boys keep it for me till I homestead up here?" he asked, giving the bell a little shake.

A lump came up in my throat. I knew it was his gentle way of saying there might not be another goodbye.

Chapter Fourteen

Greener Pastures

How could time disappear so quickly? It had been four years since we had begun our homesteading adventure—not easy years, for sure, but good years for me. I had learned so much! Now I was eighteen—grown-up. I needed to make some serious choices about my life. Our promised land wasn't exactly overflowing with milk and honey at this point. In fact, it was a combined family effort to just survive. My meager earnings as mail carrier and winter trapper, in addition to picking up odd jobs did not inspire me to take that as my lifework. I needed to expand my horizons.

Paul and Mary had moved to Carrot River, a town almost 250 miles away. Paul was working as a forest ranger. Maybe there would be more opportunity for work over there. My trusty Model T would take me to check things out, but I better head out before winter set in.

It was past midnight by the time I reached Carrot River, and I had a problem—where did they live? They weren't expecting me, and it was a new town for me. My clue to go by was that Paul owned a car. Fortunately, the town was not large and not many people owned cars. I drove across the tracks to the edge of town . . . Ah, that looked like a car Paul might choose. I decided to try that house.

The windows were all dark, but when I tried the door, it was unlocked. I opened it just a little way. Immediately, I recognized the scent of lavender. Mary loved lavender, and their homes in Pierceland and Goodsoil had that same faint, sweet smell. Then I heard the tick-tock of their mantle clock. I stepped inside and was feeling around for a couch to lie down on when Paul's deep voice called out, "Who's there?"

"John."

"Come right on in," he boomed.

The next morning, Paul assured me he could keep me busy while I looked for something better. More often than not, I helped with their farming, but I also sometimes helped him cruise timber. My axe had a number stamp on the back that I used to stamp the trees to be cut.

Sometimes Mary felt the urge to get out, so I would saddle up a couple of horses and we'd go out riding, just like old times.

By now, they had a little duffer, Don. We had a special bond. One time, Don was riding with his mom and dad; I was following in my Model T far enough back to avoid the dust. I guess he decided he wanted to ride with Uncle John, because they stopped and let him off. I could see him far ahead, waiting for me in his little coat, hoping I would stop for him. I helped him in, and he sat very straight, proud to be riding with me. No, maybe, he had a proud uncle, too.

Greener Pastures

One of the men from Mary's home Sabbath School came by one day and asked if I'd be interested in his small dairy herd. He needed out from under them, but cows just weren't selling. I could have them for thirty dollars a head.

Mary said, "I'll put the money up front, and you can pay me back."

So that's how I got into dairy farming. I started off with fourteen milkers and a deal with Paul to use some of his farmland. I was in instant business, supplying the town of just over two hundred with fresh milk. The housewives quickly knew that the milk was clean, cold, and on time.

Days began early, around 4:30 a.m., as all the work was done by hand. After milking, I quickly strained the milk and cooled it over cold, running water before bottling and delivering it. Major, my big dog, played a big role in the delivery process, and the townspeople loved him. Let me tell you a little about him.

Some years earlier, while cutting cordwood in Manitoba, I had been given a Newfoundlander pup as a thank-you for caring for the eleven-pup litter he came from. Later, he bred with Herbert's St. Bernard, and Herbert gave me Major from that litter. Major became a fine dog and a loyal worker. He and I teamed up to deliver more than five hundred pounds of milk and bottles almost every day, year round. I made a special harness for him to pull a cart in summer and a toboggan-like sled in winter. He loved this job and acted quite insulted when I thought the drifts were too high for him, hitching up a horse instead.

If a cartwheel needed repair, he would wait patiently outside the smith shop, ignoring yippy dogs and refusing to get involved in dogfights.

On the route, there was one little terrier that would dash out at him, yapping and nipping his heels. This went on for days and weeks until one day Major decided he'd had enough. He picked up the little scrapper, shook him thoroughly, and tossed him back onto his own turf. That terrier never bothered Major again.

One of my first challenges as a dairyman was to fence the land, then cross-fence it, so that I could rotate the pastures and keep them fresh and green. Besides keeping fences in good repair, looking after the cows, and milking and delivering milk, I had haying to do, in addition to cleaning the barn and other duties, but I often had the middle part of my day free to do what I wanted.

Sometimes I dropped by the stables in town to look over the horses (just like guys like to stop by car lots today). One day, I saw a beauty that stood way out ahead of even the best of them. I looked at her from every angle and decided to hang around and find out who owned her.

A smart-looking cowboy came along, and I said, "Fine horse you have there."

He agreed.

"How much would you sell her for?" I asked.

He laughed at me before answering, "She's worth more than you could ever pay, but I wouldn't sell her anyway." Then he got a glint in his eye. "Tell you what, young man. If you can ride her, you can have her."

Several fellows had gathered around by this time to listen. I didn't wait for him to change his mind. I was on her back and we were off before he could say, "Jack Robinson."

Did she give me a ride, but I stuck to her like a burr as we disappeared down the street and out of town.

Can you guess where I was heading? That's right—a swamp.

Some time later, we trotted back to the owner.

"Come on. We heard you promise!" challenged the onlookers.

The surprise and admiration on his face would have been reward enough for me, but he agreed that he had given his word.

PART II: WILDERNESS MAN

That's how I got Bess, my beautiful Canadian Hunter.

As my dairy herd grew, I decided I needed a nice big barn with a good big haymow—soon, before fall. I certainly couldn't afford to hire anyone to build it for me, and it was too much for me on my own. During the Depression, people often traded services instead of money, since money was in short supply for most of us. That's what I needed to do, but what did I have to trade, and with whom?

PART II:
WILDERNESS MAN

Chapter Fifteen

Lost

Not the Saskatchewan River—again! What was going on here? I had left the river behind about forty minutes earlier and pushed my way through brush so dense I literally had to crawl on hands and knees in places. Now, just when I thought I was through the worst of it, I was back at the river. I must have gotten disoriented and made a circle.

But what was this? The river was running to my left, and if I had circled, it should be running to my right. I couldn't figure it out, and I pinched myself to be sure I hadn't taken leave of my senses. It couldn't be, but it was a river, as swift and wide as the one I had left behind.

Never Say Whoa In A Bad Place

What could I do but turn back into that brush. This time I would be more careful and break twigs to mark my way.

How had I gotten myself into this fix?

Weeks earlier, Frank, Clarence, and Don had joined me from the homestead to help build the much-needed dairy barn, along with a friend, Pete Sawatsky. An expense-paid trip to BC in my old modified Chrysler pickup in exchange for a few weeks' work was the arrangement. Mother and Father had recently moved to the Fraser Valley along with Bill's family, and we wanted to check out their mild green paradise.

Let me tell you, we boys built a barn anyone would have been proud of, and later, we had a grand trip to the coast in my old pickup, even though it didn't have a speedometer—I would check my speed now and then by sticking my hand out the window.

In the middle of our barn project, we decided to take a break—a weekend camping trip. Mary baked and packed some tarts and beans for us, and we piled into an old Buick and headed west for the Saskatchewan River. We made camp, had supper, and decided to poke around a little before it got dark. That's when we discovered an old canoe cached by the river. It didn't look like it had been used in a while because it only had one paddle, but it was enough to get my wheels turning.

I knew that a group of Mennonite young people from McTagen area was camping upriver from us—oh, maybe five to eight miles. I had my eye on a pretty young lady from there that was with them. If we left early in the morning, we could join the group and have fun with the young people there. My brothers were game, so we planned an early start.

We must have been a sight—five big boys in one canoe in the swift Saskatchewan River current, with one paddle! We hugged the banks to avoid the strongest currents, but even then it was very slow going. We zigzagged back and forth.

The guys were very quiet. I got the feeling that no one wanted to be first to say, "Let's give up." Since I had come up with the whole idea and was the only one who felt an urgent need to continue on, I needed to come up with an alternative.

"Look," I said. "Let me off here and I'll walk straight up from the river 'til I hit the cut road. Then I'll just follow it upriver to the camp. That will lighten the load so you can make better time. And going back will be a breeze."

They were not very anxious to drop me off, but I assured them I'd be fine. It was obvious we weren't going to make it the way we were going, and I wasn't about to say whoa in a bad place. They pulled up onto the bank and let me off.

I started straight from the river and headed into the brush, and oh, there was brush! Underbrush so thick it filled me with panic. As I fought my way through, I could smell bear. The land was rolling, but with no definite hill like I had expected. I continued to push on for what seemed forever, when suddenly I broke into the open where you found me at the beginning of this chapter.

Getting my wits together, I turned back and forced myself to retrace my steps. A startled mother bear with two young cubs snorted at me and sent me shimmying up a poplar. She didn't hang around to watch. I slid back down and continued on about another half mile. Believe it or not, I found myself back at the river.

This current is going to my right. Now this is strange! I thought.

Then it hit me—I must be on an island! My ears started to pound as terror struck. I was trapped on a brush-covered bears' paradise, my brothers and the canoe were long gone, and the river was too swift to attempt a crossing, at least from here. I had to get off this island. I pulled my wits together so I could think. My best chance for the least current, I decided, would be from the down-river end of the island.

Heading back into that frightful brush, I tried to ignore the heavy bear odor that hung in the air. The branches tore at my face and hands as I pushed my way for literally hours. Just before reaching the point, I scared up a big he-bear from his vantage fishing point. He went, "Woof, woof!" and raced right past me before I could even move. I could have reached out and touched him.

Even here, the river was extremely swift, but I wasn't going back into that brush to search for a better spot. This was it! I stripped, wrapped my clothes into a tight bundle, tied them onto my back and waded out into the icy water. With the current whirling around the point of the island, it swept me off my feet. I swam hard, angling my body into the current—a technique known as "ferrying," and the current carried me straight across without even any drifting.

I was numb with cold and shaking like a leaf in a windstorm, but I had escaped the island prison of menacing bears. What a relief! Amazingly enough, my clothes were hardly wet. I gratefully scrambled into them. It wasn't long before I reached the road, actually just about where I expected. One look at the setting sun sealed the decision to head for our camp, a decision that would have been wise much earlier in the day.

I headed down the road. Darkness crept in with about a mile and a half left to go, when over a rise two headlights appeared. The approaching car slowed down. A head stuck out of the window, and a familiar voice said, "Is that you, John?"

My brothers and that old Buick had never looked so good before.

"Well, how'd your day go? Did you ever find the youth group?" I asked after I settled in.

"No, we actually turned back after we dropped you off. The current was totally impossible," Frank said. "And what about you?"

"Nope," I said. "I had you drop me off on an island, where I spent my day with the brush and the bears. It's sure a good thing I never say whoa in a bad place."

Chapter Sixteen

Moving On

Although I never reached that youth camp on the Saskatchewan River, the girl I was so intent on seeing was not forgotten. In fact, on December 24, 1940, Mary became my wife.

Now a baby was on the way. Mary, the charming girl of my dreams, deserved better than I could provide in the depression-hit town of Carrot River, Saskatchewan. I had never been afraid of change. How about moving to beautiful BC? Both my parents and Bill's family were enjoying the gentle climate and green pastures of the Fraser Valley.

I left my cows and stock with Paul and Mary since we were on their land, and we drove all the way to Ladner in the Fraser Valley—

real dairy country.

My brother Bill was milking for a large dairy, and he instantly came up with a temporary job for me. He approached his boss.

"I've never asked you for time off, but I badly need a break to build a house for my parents. I would like to ask for two weeks off."

"You know as well as I do what happens to milk production when you put a new guy in," said the owner. "It won't work, Bill. Sorry!"

"I'd like you to give my brother a try," Bill told him. "I can pretty well guarantee there'll be no drop in milk production."

He hesitated. Then, "Alright, I'll give him a try. But you be handy if it doesn't work."

I had work for the rest of the summer at one of the largest dairies in the valley. It was considered a model dairy, and visitors from far and near, even from overseas, came by to see it. Everything had to be shipshape. My Mary kept the stone milkhouse spotless and shining, but our first baby was on the way.

Before the end of the season, I had lined up a job in a health food bakery for an Adventist fellow in Victoria—Hubert Bailey was his name. I was the baker, and Hubert took care of the business end and deliveries.

So that's how Kenneth came to be born in Victoria, November 10, 1941.

Donalda was born almost two years later. About that time, I bought my own bakery in Ocean Falls on the coast. Rueben and his wife Pat lived there, and my younger brothers logged in the area for the Gildersleeves.

Although the town was small, the war gave it quite a boom. A lot of ships stopped in port, along with a few sailors.

I remember a few young fellows dropping by to shoot the breeze.

Never Say Whoa In A Bad Place

"You've got it pretty soft," one of the guys teased. "Baking is sissy work."

"Maybe," I said, dumping a hundred-pound batch of dough out on the worktable. I picked up the dough and put it down again. "Here, lift this."

He confidently stepped up to the table, but that dough would not cooperate. He'd get one part only to lose the rest. His friend came to help, but it wasn't much better.

I think they gained a new respect for bakers and dough.

I was proud of the bread, rolls, and pies I turned out. (I always used a broom handle to roll out my pastry.)

Marilyn joined our family on the first day of spring in 1945, just before the end of World War II. A few months later, my wife left our three children and me. I felt like my world had collapsed.

For more than three years, I hoped and prayed we would be reunited. I would occasionally take the children and go to visit her. It was no easy job to try to keep the children together while I worked to support them.

Mary finally asked me for a divorce so she could marry again.

I moved to Langley during the divorce so that Mother could help me with the children. I was determined to keep my children together and live under one roof.

I needed a temporary job to put bread on the table.

"Cab drivers needed," read the sign on the taxi stand.

Why not try? I applied and walked out of the office with a smart dark olive-green uniform and a new job.

Over the next few months, I got to know my way around Vancouver very well. I also learned a lot more about people—turning down brassy women in the red-light districts, getting fares from obnoxious drunks, and even delivering a baby who refused to wait for his mother to get to the hospital. (Lucky for me I had driven the horses for Mother while she worked as a midwife in Flat Valley.)

Once, on my way back from Vancouver, this fellow kept passing me, cutting me off, then slowing way down to force me to pass him so he could repeat his performance. I don't know if he just had it in for cabbies or if he needed some amusement, but it was wasting my time, and he wasn't tiring of his little game.

Finally, I decided to pay tit for tat. He cut in front of me and slowed right down. I immediately pulled out, passed him, and cut in front of him very short, so short, in fact, that my back bumper caught his front bumper and spun his car 180 degrees. That was back when bumpers weren't just for looks.

Fortunately, no damage was done, and he left me alone after that.

The divorce was a low point in my life, but it was time to move on. Never say whoa in a bad spot. So I opened my eyes and saw this feisty little redhead in church. Jean came from Low German stock, just like me, and she was about my age. I began courting her.

She worked in Langley, staying with her sister and family, the Dalkes, out on Livingston Road. She ordinarily rode the bus to and from work, but if it were at all convenient, I'd pick her up in my cab and take her home after work.

Months later, I had a couple in the backseat of my cab, but I swung by Jean's bus stop, and sure enough, she was there. I pulled over, and she opened the door and hopped in. We had just recently gotten engaged, and she slid over and cuddled up to me. I figured she hadn't seen the passengers in the backseat since it was already dark, so I quietly told her in Low German that there were people in the backseat.

Apparently she didn't hear what I said, because she cuddled up even closer and said, "I just can't get close enough."

Never Say Whoa In A Bad Place

I repeated myself a little louder. This time she got it. Poor Jean! She was so embarrassed!

"Let me off. Let me off," she demanded, sliding to the other end of the seat and opening the door. I had to stop quickly.

The couple in the back enjoyed the whole thing. "You don't need to take us to the theatre after all. We already got to watch the show," they told me.

Chapter Seventeen

Colporteur

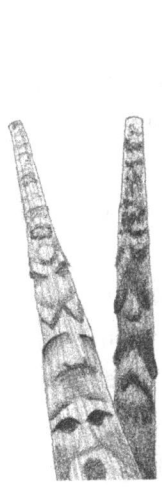

I married Jean in July of 1949. And so began a new and rewarding family life, and also a new line of work.

I didn't return to the bakery. I didn't think it was healthy to be working in high temperatures from early till late, constantly breathing in flour dust. Cab driving had served its purpose as a short-term fill-in, but I needed to be outdoors, I decided.

BC is known for its forests and its logging industry. I got started by cutting and sawing railroad ties and trucking them to Bellingham, Washington.

We went to Hope Camp Meeting the next summer and were in-

Never Say Whoa In A Bad Place

spired with the colporteurs' reports. Jean had loved selling books to earn her tuition for Canadian Union College, a Christian boarding school, when she became an Adventist. She enthusiastically encouraged me to enter the Lord's work selling Christian books.

We returned home to pack up and move to Terrace, my field of labor. Ron Reimche worked in the same district, which included Terrace, the Hazeltons, Smithers, and all the outlying areas between. There were a few native reservations, but all in all, the population was pretty sparse.

I enjoyed my work, especially meeting the people. On Sundays and in the evenings, I worked on building a small, two-story house on a piece of land up on the bench above Terrace. There was a little church school within walking distance for the children. It was almost too good to be true—and it was.

About that time the conference changed its policy for literature evangelists. We now had to buy our stock to sell. Our meager earnings were burned up in gas, traveling the many miles between homes.

I moved the family to Kitwanga, a small Indian village across the Skeena River, which was more central to my district. We lived in an old house behind a sawmill. I was away from home for a week or two at a time, camping out. This meant that I left Jean with the children, which now included little Bonnie, with no car, and of course, no phone. This was not ideal, but we were doing the Lord's work.

I made good friends with the native chiefs in the area. When the salmon were running, one of my new friends brought us several huge fish and insisted on giving them to us as a gift. We canned and canned salmon, and what a blessing it was that winter.

In Hot Water

One Friday evening, I arrived home late. The children were already upstairs in bed. Jean met me at the door. "You've got a sick girl upstairs. She burned her foot badly in the sawdust pile over a week ago, and its looking bad. I'm glad you're home, because I don't know what to do."

"Stoke the fire, and get the hot water going," I instructed before heading upstairs to get Donalda.

I had warned the children two months ago not to play in the sawdust pile anymore, because it was being burned. I had explained how the fire goes underground and burns caves that can trap you. Apparently, they thought the fire had gone out—Kenneth was usually so dependable, but of course, the girls got out of school an hour ahead of him.

I carried her downstairs. The entire top of her foot was a raw, open sore. It stank! Rolling up her pajamas, I saw angry streaks up her leg. My heart sank. A doctor was nowhere close, and anyhow, he would probably want to amputate. That was not going to happen if I could help it.

With a prayer in my heart, I set to work with a God-given remedy—water. I got two buckets, one for hot and one for cold.

"This is going to hurt for a while," I told my frightened eight-year-old.

She screamed as I put her foot into the hot water. I held her close, but I made her keep her foot in there for three minutes. Then I dipped her foot into the cold water for half a minute. Back and forth, back and forth, for close to an hour, I stuck her foot in the hot and cold water. Jean added hot water from the boiling kettle as I slowly increased the temperature. After the first few dips, her foot became numb so she couldn't even feel it.

I stayed home for about a week until she was well on the road to recovery. Her foot was scarred, but it was saved.

Chapter Eighteen

Niche Found

By spring I knew I could not support my family by selling books. We moved back to our home in Terrace, and I joined a group of young fallers out toward Stewart. From then on, I was a logger, with just a few temporary detours.

The climate was kind of coastal in that area with lots of large trees and underbrush and more than enough mosquitoes. To start with, we camped in tents.

We had just moved camp one Friday, when the fellows decided they were heading home for the weekend.

"We can't leave all this stuff unattended," I said. "I'll stay," I told them.

Niche Found

They left, and I puttered around, setting up shelves and getting things organized. I didn't have time to put up any bunks, so I just made a comfy bed with spruce boughs.

Sabbath was a beautiful day. I studied my Sabbath School lesson, took a nice walk, and ate lunch. A good time to stretch out and take a rest, I decided. The day was so pleasant that I tied back the tent flaps before I climbed into my sleeping bag and zipped it up. Ahh! It feels so good. Sabbath is special anywhere, I thought.

In semi-consciousness, I suddenly became aware of a dimly familiar smell. Opening my eyes, I noticed the tent was starting to sway. I made a quick room check. There he was—a full-grown black bear. Now, black bears are not all that big, but in that tent, he looked as big as a horse!

I didn't want to scare him and have him take the whole tent down, but he was coming my way, sniffing and snuffing curiously.

I'll tell him I'm here, I decided. I tried, but my voice wasn't working. I tried again, managing to get out a low grunt.

The bear gathered his legs under him and made the neatest turn-on-a-dime maneuver I've ever seen, and out he went.

I was out of my sleeping bag in a jiffy! I got those tent flaps tied down before he could change his mind and come back.

By Sunday night, the guys still weren't back. I tied the flaps down and turned in for the night. Hmm, I heard an animal approaching. This time, I was ready.

"Mr. Bear, I'm here!" I called in a no-nonsense voice.

"Thump, thump, thump!" came the reply on the plywood outside my door.

Every time I said something, I got that "thump, thump, thump" response.

My curiosity got the better of me. I got up and peeked out the flaps where the bear should have been. Nothing!

My glance traveled downward. Yes, there was something, but much lower down. In the moonlight, I could see something dark with two white stripes. The skunk's tail was actually up against the tent. I VERY quietly stepped back and slipped into my sleeping bag. I would let my visitor leave on his own terms.

As our group of fallers got better organized, we scouted around and found some better logging areas available at Babine Lake, the longest natural lake in the province. We could drive as far as Topley Landing then cross by boat to our camp. We built cabins and moved our families, making a nice little Adventist camp, consisting of the McCreerys, Blabeys, Thompsons, our family, and a couple of college students.

Jean was happy about the social aspect and fellowship, but the water was a different story. She dreaded every crossing. A storm could blow in so fast, and I'll admit those four-foot whitecaps could look pretty high above our boat. I'd keep the bow headed into the waves, while Jean and the children bailed. We never swamped; not everyone was so fortunate.

Bonnie did not share her mother's fear of water and would toddle right into the lake, shoes and all, and keep right on going.

Donalda and Marilyn got into collecting bugs and butterflies of many sizes and colors. In fact, they were so serious about it that I picked up some chloroform so they could put their specimens "to sleep" without damaging their beautiful wings.

Kenneth had a fascination with machinery, and he spent time making friends with the cat operator.

And of course, yours truly was cutting timber out with the mosquitoes and no-see-ums.

Niche Found

I remember an old-timer in the area who was still using a Swede saw for cutting trees. He figured the smoke from our chainsaws helped keep the little biters at bay.

"But me—My saw say 'Zing, zing!' Me call dem!" he told us.

One day I made my undercut, then sawed through from the other side, and yelled, "Timber!" Down it came.

As I topped the tree and started limbing it, I saw the hole and the tiny face of a baby flying squirrel. The mother and brothers or sisters were gone. I couldn't leave the little orphan. I tucked him safely in my shirt pocket and took him home.

The whole family was delighted. Jean warmed up a little canned milk and fed him with an eyedropper. He also loved peanut butter.

"We can all enjoy him," I said. "But he will be Kenneth's special responsibility."

They took to each other like peaches and cream. Kenneth nailed a little box above his bed and made a soft little nest for his miniature pet. Before Jean and I would turn in for the night, we'd check the box. More often then not, it was empty. The first time that happened, we hunted high and low. Finally, we pulled back Kenneth's quilt to find the squirrel had climbed down and nestled close to his master. After that, we knew where to look. Somehow, Kenneth never rolled over it.

Flying squirrels are gentle, timid creatures. We don't often see them because they hide out during the day. But they become very affectionate pets if treated kindly.

Chapter Nineteen

Accident at Babine Lake

One fine August morning in 1952, as we were spooning in our porridge, Kenneth asked, "Daddy, can I ride the cat today? The driver said it's OK with him."

I didn't feel easy about it, and so I sat thinking for a moment.

"Please, Daddy. It goes so slowly, and I'll be careful. What could go wrong?"

I thought a moment longer. I somehow didn't like the idea. Yet he was right. He was careful, and so was the cat operator.

"Maybe," I said. "Get Mommy to pack you a lunch, and we'll go over and talk to the operator."

When we reached the job site, he greeted us with a smile. "My nephew's coming too," the operator told us.

As I turned to leave, a delighted Kenneth dug into his lunch bucket and pulled out his orange.

"Here, Daddy, take it," he urged. "I won't need it."

Seeing how much he wanted to say thank you, I smiled and took it.

Unfortunately, just a few hours later, I saw Verne Gustafson running toward me. I turned off my saw. "There's been an accident . . ." he panted.

He didn't need to say any more. My heart stood still, but I followed him back to the cat, where the fellows were preparing a litter to carry my son back to camp.

I gently lifted his broken body and carried him to an empty cabin, where I cleaned and dressed him myself before I called his sisters to say their goodbyes. Then we took his body to Terrace for the funeral.

As the story unfolded, I discovered that the younger boy was driving, and the cat operator had turned his attention elsewhere. The boy forgot how to stop the caterpillar, so Kenneth stepped across to help him. His leather bootlace had come undone and got caught in the track. The lace was too strong to break loose, and Kenneth was pulled through where the blade attaches to the cat. By the time the cat operator was aware and stopped the machine, it was too late.

Kenneth's young friend was so distraught that in the aftermath of the accident he ran and hid. He was sure he would be punished as a murderer, so we had a lost boy on our hands as well for a few hours.

It was a dark hour. Along with this gaping hole in my life, I was fighting the fear of being charged as an unfit father and losing Donalda and Marilyn as well.

Some experiences are too hard to understand. That's when we need to know that there's a God of love out there. He sees the whole picture and will work out even the blackest night into something good. God let me know that I would not choose to be led otherwise if I could see the end from the beginning, like He can.

Kenneth was buried on the bench above Terrace in sight of the home I had built there. One day soon, he'll hear a trumpet, and he'll wake up to find that his wish to be a child when Christ returns has come true. Kenneth loved the Lord with all his heart. He was ready.

Red Bluff Camp

In our close-knit little camp, every family was devastated. It was about time to get a new start, so we moved our operation to Red Bluff Camp across the lake.

On one of my return trips to pick up another load of goods from our first camp, I noticed a kitten acting strangely. She walked with her head kind of bent to one side.

We had been overrun with mice. Hearing about our problem when we were in Terrace, a friend had given us a mother cat and her two kittens to help out the camp.

"She's an excellent mouser," we were promised, and she was. But what was the problem with the kitten?

I picked her up and checked her neck, then her mouth. Oh, oh! She had a fishhook planted inside her cheek. Apparently, she must have seen the shiny spoon on the end of a fishing line, and in playing with it, gotten the hook embedded in her mouth. She couldn't eat or drink. She wasn't about to let me touch it, but I couldn't let her go like this.

I suddenly remembered the girls' chloroform for their bugs. Was it still here? Sure enough, the little bottle still sat on a high shelf. How much chloroform does it take to put a kitten to sleep before it's too much? I wondered. I set to work.

Soon the hook was removed. I set out a saucer of milk and waited.

Accident at Babine Lake

My patient woke up, got up on wobbly feet, and tottered over to the saucer to join her mother and brother. Once she got some warm milk in her tummy, she was set to go again.

From our new camp, we could actually see Topley Landing. We were set back in a somewhat protected cove, where we had our log boom. We did not have a mill, so we cut logs and stored them in a boom until a tug would come and pull the whole boom to a sawmill. It was of vital importance to keep the boom shipshape, but even then, a fierce storm sometimes broke it.

Sometimes in the middle of the night, we would hear the wind pick up, the waves dashing on the shore, and the logs jostling one against the other, louder and louder. If the boom broke, the whole cove was a mass of dark, writhing bodies, like a maddened herd of wild buffalo. The BOOM, BOOM of the crashing logs kept the whole camp awake.

There was nothing to do but wait out the storm, for our small boats would have been smashed like toothpicks out there.

Then began the round up. We would have to travel up and down the lake, looking for our brand—every logging outfit had their own stamp, and every log was stamped. And of course there were many other boats out on the lake doing the same thing as we were. It was a major job to recoup a boomful of logs, and we did everything in our power to prevent a break.

Once, on a log round up, I noticed an old canoe on shore. I turned in to check it out. Would you believe it, I had found an honest-to-goodness dugout canoe. A tree had fallen and clipped off the bow, but otherwise, it was sound.

The next evening, I brought Donalda and Marilyn to see my treasure. They rode in it while I towed it home for them (backwards, so it wouldn't take on water). They loved to play Indians in it.

Never Say Whoa In A Bad Place

Meanwhile, I had my ear to the ground for a different job. It just wasn't fair to Jean to stay here at Babine. Familiarity with that lake was not helping; every crossing was a nightmare for her.

Around Christmastime I received a letter from Mary and Paul. Paul was setting up a mill west of Dawson Creek. Would I come and be in charge of the falling? Perhaps this was the answer I was looking for.

Early spring saw us loading up our belongings and heading off on a new adventure.

Chapter Twenty

A Brush with Death

We arrived and set up camp in Sunshine Valley, near Progress. We built a cookhouse, a row of cabins, a bunkhouse, and off a ways, the sawmill. Paul looked after the mill crew, and I, the fallers and skidders. Jean helped Mary in the cookhouse. School-age children took correspondence lessons. We had a nice setup and a good Christian crew.

Several months later, Jean's sister, Naomi, and her three children, Christine, Niel, and Glenn, arrived, needing a home. We found larger lodgings out of camp, at the Miners and then at the Hollys, a large vacant log house. (It was quite a grand house, built by a rich American rancher, with extensive barns and outbuildings. Their animals were hit with hoof-and-mouth disease, and all of them had to be destroyed. The Hollys declared bankruptcy and returned to the States.) With a big barrel heater to keep us warm, it made a wonderful refuge for our enlarged family for close to a year. There was plenty of room for them to romp, indoors and out. (The banister provided a ride on the sly on more than one occasion, I'm sure.) At the foot of the hill on the highway was Groner's Store and across from it, a one-room school for the three older girls to attend.

I liked working in the bush falling trees, and pardon me for saying so, but I was good at it. I like to see a job well done. The work was not the problem, but the money end of things was not working out as expected. The bill for groceries at Groner's Store was adding up, in spite of our moose-meat and venison.

I kept working, hoping that things would come around through the winter. Times were pretty tough! It was time to spy out the land farther south, I decided.

Down in Kamloops, I learned about homesteads opening up around Adams Lake. I checked it out—beautiful wild country, rich soil, wild hay up to my waist, and huge, healthy mosquitoes for free. It truly was a land flowing with milk and honey, enough to make me dizzy with dreams. But by now, I knew Jean would not share my pioneering enthusiasm.

Using common sense, I headed on to Vernon. Herman Kneller was setting up a logging operation above Lavington, between Vernon and Lumby—the same Kneller that homesteaded with our family years earlier in Flat Valley. His older brothers, Dan and Rueben, were with him. I signed up, and so did my twin brother.

I found a place to rent and drove back to fetch my big family. With

A Brush with Death

the truck loaded high, I led the way, letting the children take turns riding with me. Jean and Naomi followed in the car with the rest of the family. Back then the road was gravel almost the whole way. It was a long trip, and I wiled away the hours singing old songs to entertain the children. They were quite impressed with my yodeling—something I hadn't tried since my boyhood. They were such good travelers that I decided to reward them with a hot meal.

We stopped at a restaurant. There wasn't much money, but I ordered everyone a bowl of hot soup. Did I say hot? I never tasted hotter! There was so much black pepper in it that no one could eat it, although Naomi and I tried.

We went back to our zwieback, and carried on, stopping only for gas or to stretch a leg and exchange passengers. We traveled likt this all the way to Monte Lake. It was already dark, and we were ready for a break. I pulled in and rented a cabin.

The next morning, I showed the children how to skip rocks on the water, before pulling out for the last short leg of the journey.

A few months later, Naomi gave birth to a baby boy. Because of her situation, she had agreed to let Jean and me raise it as our own. Little Johnny would help fill Kenneth's place.

But that was not to be. Somehow welfare got involved, and they literally pried the baby out of Jean's arms to put him in a foster home.

Less than a year later, in November of 1955, our own son was born—Leander. God is good!

Christine, Niel, and Glenn continued to be part of our family on and off again for the next ten years, and to this day they hold a special place for me.

After a while Herman decided to move his logging operation

north, but Jean was not ready to move north. So I picked up a temporary falling job behind Vernon toward Silver Star, close to the dam. One evening, a fellow batching near me came by, and we went for a walk. As we walked, we exchanged a few loggers' tales. His little mongrel was running ahead, occupying himself with squirrel and rabbit trails.

Suddenly, we heard, "Yip! Yip!" from far ahead; soon, "Yip! Yip!" again, a little closer.

"Yip! Yip!" From around the corner and down the hill raced the little dog. Gaining on him was a full-grown cougar. It sprang!

"Yip! Yip!" Fido tucked in his tail and ran even faster. If only he could reach his master in time!

The cougar was so intent on the dog that he hadn't noticed us. I better do something, I thought. I clapped sharply, waved my arms, and hollered, "Hey!"

The cougar applied his brakes and skidded to a stop in the gravel not more than six feet in front of us. We had a good look at each other before he sprang into the ditch and disappeared in the brush.

Brown's Logging in the Merritt area offered me a job. Pay was good and working conditions easier—less brush and less snow. The downside was that I was away from the family all week, and the crew was pretty rough and crude, but we needed the money for the girls to attend school. (Grade eight math by correspondence was beyond Jean's comfort zone, so living in logging camps was out for the family since Donalda and Marilyn needed to be in school.)

A year or so later when my friend Floyd Smith asked me to team up with him, I was ready to listen. He did the milling, I did the falling and skidding, and his brother George, the trucking. It meant going into debt for a new skidder, but the money and job were good.

A Brush with Death

It was another day on the job. Another tree to cut. I stepped back and looked up—a straight, tall bull pine, typical of the area. I made the undercut, sawed through from the other side, stepped back, and watched it lean into the undercut and silently fall.

A sturdy protruding branch hit the ground first, turning the angle of the tree and catapulting it backwards. The butt caught me full in the chest, pinning me to another tree and knocking the breath out of me. I heard my ribs popping. My angel must have stopped that log from crushing the life out of me on the spot.

There was no one near to call for help. Camp was almost three miles away, and no one would be expecting me before evening. There weren't a whole lot of options to consider, and besides, just trying to breathe was enough of a challenge. I passed out briefly. Coming to, I prayed, "Lord, if it's Your will for me, You can get me out of this. But if not, may I be ready to meet You when You come."

I passed out again. When I came to, I tried to figure out a way to leave a message for my family. In my shirt pocket was my record notebook, which was locked in the same giant vice that held me prisoner, but with effort, I extracted the pen. Now for something to write on. How about my shirtsleeve? I tried to reach across the top of the log with my left arm . . . Made it!

Dearest Jean, I wrote, I love you. I am ready to go, and I look forward to seeing you when Jesus comes. Love the children for me. John.

That done, I focused on staying alert. I didn't think I would wake up again this side of eternity if I fainted again.

"Lord," I prayed, "I don't think it's a selfish request to save me for my family, if it's Your will . . ."

Did I feel the log move slightly? Sure enough, it moved again, this time just enough for me to slip out. Somehow, I walked back to the mill. Floyd's family had come to spend Easter break at the camp with him. As I approached the mill on the skidding trail, holding my chest, his son Melvin spotted me first. I just said, "It hurts!" and he shot off for help.

If I thought the walk to camp was torture, I don't know what to call the thirty-mile ride in the back of the pickup over rough logging roads to the hospital. Even though Floyd's wife, Alberta, put down blankets for me and Floyd did his best to miss the worst of the potholes, it was still torture. Alberta sat in the back with me, and she later recounted that I stopped breathing several times. But God hadn't gotten me out of that trap to have me die on the road.

Once at the hospital, X-rays showed multiple fractures to all my ribs except for three lower ones. In addition, both collarbones were broken.

No more falling trees for me for a few years, but I was alive!

Chapter Twenty-One

A Woolly Detour to Wild Horses

The logging accident in the Merritt-Spences Bridge area in 1958 brought about an abrupt change in my life. With almost every rib and both collarbones sustaining multiple fractures, I was not able to continue falling or skidding.

I allowed my partner to use the skidder I had purchased in exchange for keeping up the payments, but it didn't pan out. Not only was my equipment repossessed, but we lost our family car to the company as well.

With no transportation, I couldn't get to town for my doctor's appointment, so I was cut off of compensation just a few months after the accident. I could see that without a lawyer the Workmen's Compensation Board was more than I could fight. And there was no money for a lawyer.

I had a family to feed. There was no time to say whoa!

As soon as I was on my feet, I started job-hunting, but I didn't have a whole lot to offer. Physical activity was painful and limited. Less than three years of education was also limiting. But experience . . . Well, I had a fair amount of that. And I was comfortable around animals.

I checked out the Nichola Stock Farms and was promptly hired as a shepherd. It wasn't good pay, but it was better than nothing.

I was off to a busy start, for it was lambing season. Growing up on the farm prepared me to handle many different emergencies, like skinning a stillborn lamb to cover a triplet from another ewe so the ewe with no lamb would allow it to suckle. I had no "bum lambs."

One ewe forced out a lot of her intestines along with her afterbirth. I washed them up as best I could and tucked them back inside. Believe it or not, she survived.

A summer of herding sheep in the hills followed. I batched in a little trailer that the ranch provided.

That fall, I learned that one of their flocks in the valley was in trouble. Because the ground was too wet for them on the lowlands, the sheep had developed hoof rot. Nichola Farms was planning to put down about three hundred bred ewes, only because of their bad feet. I figured they could be saved with a bit of work, so I talked to the manager.

Yes, I could have the whole flock for a thousand dollars. But where could I come up with that kind of money? If I could partner with someone who had the money, I would do the work. The ewes were already bred, so the investment would be a hard one to lose on.

A Woolly Detour to Wild Horses

My friend, John Weir, took me on. One-third of the ewes were mine for my work.

I quickly set to work. I made a shallow dip with a creosote mixture that the ewes had to be driven through. It was nasty stuff, but it worked after repeated treatments. By lambing time, the ewes' hooves were healed.

Now, what does this have to do with wild horses?

Our two oldest, Donalda and Marilyn, were boarding in Merritt to go to school. When the summer of 1960 rolled around, they came home to a two-room cabin in the middle of nowhere that was already bulging with five of us. Something needed to happen.

I had the sheep out to summer pasture by this time. The night corral was set up, the bothersome bears were mostly dealt with, our Alsatian was a good herder and good company, and there was a tent to sleep in. Sheepherding would be a good experience for the girls. They would be sort of roughing it, and in the meantime learning to cope with a wider education than what's in a textbook. Once a week I could check on them and bring in supplies.

The girls were game.

Soon, I had caught up with the odd jobs around home. I was pretty good friends with the Indians on the reserve at the foot of the mountain where our logging road joined the highway between Merritt and Spences Bridge. Old John Snow, a friend of mine, had told me about some wild horse bands farther back in the hills.

It's an ill wind that doesn't blow something good for someone, they say. This unaccustomed break from work provided an opportunity too good to waste.

I headed for the hills to find the whereabouts and makeup of the different bands.

Wild Horses

Crawling on my hands and knees toward the brow of the rise, I hoped to get a better view of the band of wild horses I had been tracking since morning. I had dismounted and left my saddle horse downwind in a draw so that I could approach unobserved. Suddenly, my horse whinnied.

There was an immediate challenging scream from the stallion. His thundering hooves told me he was headed our way.

This was not good. As the pounding hooves came closer, I reached for the gun on my back and stood up to meet him.

He entered my sights—nostrils flared, teeth bared, broad-chested, roan—but there was no more time to check him over. I pulled the trigger.

BANG!

He started to turn in mid-air, and down he went; dead with one shot. I looked him over. Not as striking as the buckskin and sorrel stallions I had observed in two of the other bands in these hills, but he certainly was a lusty, healthy fellow. His thick, sturdy hooves especially caught my attention. I was sorry I had to do him in. But his six mares would soon join another band.

Now, other responsibilities called for my attention, but next spring, I'd be back. As I rode back to camp, I formulated a plan of how I would single out a couple of horses from these wild bands and catch them.

I had been out in the hills for almost a week and had found and observed seven bands of horses, anywhere from six to twelve head.

Some horsemen have said the lead mare runs the herd, others have said the stallion is boss. I decided both were right from my observations. The lead mare was usually the oldest and most dominant female, and she was always in the lead. But I had noticed that when the band

A Woolly Detour to Wild Horses

was running, the mare turned according to the stallion's screams—a team leadership.

I liked what I saw, but I knew that I needed to patiently wait for the right time. I figured they'd be easiest to catch at the end of winter.

Spring arrived. I waited for the lower hills to green up. It had been a long winter—a hard one for the animals. I knew the horses would be coming off the mountains to get fresh fodder, and they would not be in prime shape (to my advantage).

It was now or never.

"Jean," I said to my wife, "I'd like to take me a holiday. I'll be gone for at least a week, and I expect to bring back a horse or two." I sketched out my plan to her.

I loaded my tent and sleeping bag, hatchet, bucket, skillet, and matches—you know, camping basics. Then came the equipment for catching my horses: three long lariats, about fifteen rolls of toilet paper, and a couple of hobbles. That's right—ropes and toilet paper! Simple? You bet.

I approached from the Ashcroft side so I could make base camp close to both a road and the hills where I expected to find the horses.

By nine o'clock the next morning, I chased up a herd. They knew I was there, and they started working their way back to a higher elevation. I kept trailing them right up to the snow level, when they started to make a wide arc. I had expected that. They swung to make about a ten-mile circle. As they circled again, I prepared for them. I knew I had no choice of horses. If I got any, it would have to be the lead mare, even if I might prefer one of the younger mares.

First, I set a snare with one of my lariats just a little to the side of their trail. Then I poked the end of a long stick through a long ribbon of toilet paper and stuck it right where the trail took a turn. That would surprise the lead mare as she came around the corner, and it would turn her into my snare if things went according to plan. I knew I'd lose the rest of the band, and I'd have to work very fast to save the captured mare from hurting herself.

I hid nearby and waited. Sure enough, I could hear them coming down the trail. Was I ready?

The instant she cantered into view, the mare spotted the fluttering white paper. She veered to the left, barely snagging the snare. Down she went! The stallion screamed and turned the herd. I paid no attention to the fleeing horses.

The mare was caught by a back foot and her tail—there was no chance of her strangling herself. I had her feet trussed up before she even knew what happened, giving her no opportunity to strike at me. I quickly untied the snare, attached hobbles, and secured her to a tree before untying her feet.

It had worked more smoothly than I could have hoped for.

Of course, now came the job of turning this wild fury into something I could ride back to camp that night, but I figured correctly that the biggest challenge was already won.

You can always tell when a fighting horse submits. She drops her head, turns an ear, and chews. Then I know she's ready for the next step.

I remained up there for two weeks, catching another two horses from two other bands—three mares in all. (The first band took off to the hills. I didn't spot them again.)

Well, I loaded up my mares and set off for home. At Cache Creek, I had to stop at a checkpoint. The guy came out to check my load.

"Your horses got brands?" he asked.

"No, sir."

"Are they yours?"

"Yes, sir."

"They're looking pretty rough."

"Yes, sir. They wintered on the range. I herded sheep there last summer."

"Take care," he said, and waved me on.

It wasn't until several years later that I learned of the government's decision to destroy the wild-horse bands. To my knowledge, every horse in those hills was shot. I was glad for the three I caught. As far as I know, they or their offspring are still being used.

Chapter Twenty-Two

A Found Stallion and a Lost Girl

While still herding sheep in the Merritt area, I picked up two saddle horses from the Nicola Stock Farms: Flicka, a tall, flighty bay thoroughbred, green broke; and Queenie, a sturdier bay quarter horse who had been used for cutting cattle. Surely they would add interest and ease to sheepherding, for our herd had grown to about 700 from our initial 300. (It is not rare for sheep to bear twins and sometimes even triplets, in which case I would arrange an adoption to avoid a bum lamb, or orphan.)

I'll never forget one of my first experiences with Flicka. She was pretty high strung, and I figured she needed a bit of work. I saddled her up, led her around a bit, and swung myself up in her stirrup. You

A Found Stallion and a Lost Girl

would have thought I had planted a burr under her saddle. What a bronco she would have made for the rodeos! Away sailed my hat! When I saw her heels over my head, I decided it was time to jump.

"Young lady, you're going to learn to keep your feet on the ground," I told her, and she did. She never repeated that performance. Even my girls could ride her.

That fall we moved the sheep and all to a ranch on the Chase Creek Cutoff between Chase and Falkland. The previous owner had his horse up for sale—the most beautiful, young bay stallion I had ever laid eyes on, an Anglo-Arab. His registered name was Ebb Tide, but he went by Chief. He had the fine features and head of the Arab with a white star and white socks, and he carried himself as a king.

I couldn't remember wanting a horse so badly since I was a kid. But I was a middle-aged father of five, and I was still recuperating from a logging accident. Where was my common sense? But I had two fine mares to raise his colts, and stud fees would help him earn his keep. I reasoned back and forth. Finally, heart won out, and Chief provided years of use and pleasure. His gentle, affectionate nature never ceased to amaze me. I was never afraid to show him in the Armstrong fairs or parades.

I bided my time at the sheep ranch, but I was feeling more and more like my old self again. The sheep were keeping bread and potatoes on the table, but very little more. I started logging a little timber off the place to get me back in shape and add a few dollars for groceries.

Lost Girl

Lost girl! The news spread through the valley like wildfire and sent a chill through me. She was only eight—about half way between Bonnie and Leander in age.

Never Say Whoa In A Bad Place

She had gone with her family to spend a day at Pillar Lake, a few miles past our place. When it was time to head home, she was nowhere to be found. When they contacted the police, it was announced on the radio.

"I might be able to help," I told Jean, thinking of my experience in tracking animals. "I'll head up there and see."

The police had things well organized, and they gave me an area to comb. It was getting dark when the signal shot was given. We returned to base, but no little girl.

"Pardon me for saying so, but I think she's on the creek somewhere," I ventured.

The head honcho raised an eyebrow. "That creek is too high, and it runs through thick brush. It's too tough to follow, and anyhow, it's getting too dark to see. We'll continue the search in the morning with dogs."

We all headed for our vehicles. Some suspected that she had drowned, but I couldn't let it rest at that. There was a girl out there in light clothing, and the nights were cold. It's almost an instinct for a lost person to follow a waterway downstream. Besides, she would know that this creek came out at Chase, I reasoned. The least I could do was try.

I drove home, picked up a gas lantern, and asked Jean to set a lamp in the window on the creek side of the house. Then I headed back to Pillar Lake and started following Chase Creek. No doubt about it, the brush was dense, with fallen trees crisscrossing every which way. The spring runoff had formed logjams here and there. But I picked up tracks—a child's tracks—here and there. Where the going got too tangled, she entered the creek and kept on going. I could see the indentations in the coarse sand of the creek bed by some of the bends. There were deep spots. I prayed for her safety.

A Found Stallion and a Lost Girl

On and on I pushed, even past our place. I could see the light Jean had put in the window, but fear must have kept the child from seeking help, because her tracks continued downstream—over logs, around obstacles—I don't know how she did it in the dark, other than with her guardian angel.

Her tracks in the creek were getting more distinct. I must be catching up. I called her name now and then.

Suddenly, there she was within the circle of my light, hiding in a thicket, shaking in her shorts and summer top. I don't know how to describe how I felt—it was way beyond relief.

Fear was written all over her face. I smiled, and said reassuringly, "I can take you home. You're cold. Here, would you like to wear my jacket?"

I slipped off my jacket, and she let me wrap it around her. I picked her up and headed toward the road above the creek. I knew there was a bachelor living not too far from there.

He was pretty surprised to get a knock on his door that time of night.

I asked, "May we come in and get warmed up?"

He agreed to drive us to the girl's home. The strangest thing happened when we got there. Before I even reached for the door handle, he announced in a challenging voice, "I will take her to the door!"

We have a hopeful hero here, I thought, but out loud I said pleasantly, "Certainly, as you wish."

Did he think I was going to put up a fight? That little girl had had enough trauma for that day, and the whole point was to get her home, safe and sound.

Some time later, I met her mother in Chase. I introduced myself, and told her, "I'm the fellow who found your daughter in the creek."

She looked at me angrily as if she didn't believe me. Or maybe she thought I was going to ask for a reward.

I didn't push it any further, but I still wish I could have kept contact with that little girl. A long night of searching had developed almost a father-bond. Maybe that helps me understand how God feels about us.

Sheepherding had kept the wolf from our door, but not a whole lot more. I was ready to work in the bush again. Donalda and Marilyn had already flown the nest. Jean's heart was set on the three younger children attending a Christian school, which meant a cabin in the woods wouldn't cut it. We bought a farm on Grandview Flats, near Armstrong, as a home base.

We sold all the livestock except for Chief and two of his fillies, Bright Robin and Red Robin, both sorrels with white blazes and socks.

Bonnie was entering her teens and was a chip off the old block when it came to enjoying horses, so she kind of kept that end of things while I was away during the week.

Chapter Twenty-Three

Finlay Forks Adventures

There were a few quick "Woof, woofs" behind me . . . I recognize that sound, I thought, turning from the two men to look back up the hill.

Sure enough, two cubs were scrambling up a tree about eighty feet back, one behind the other, with the mother bear nosing the second one as if to say, "Faster, Buddy!"

"Boys, she's going to come for us," I said.

The foreman, Eddie, and Mr. Carrier, the head boss, had been showing me where they wanted me to fall next and how high the water level would be by next year. We stood about halfway between the bears and the river, where our boat was waiting below a steep drop-off.

Never Say Whoa In A Bad Place

You never saw two guys move faster, lickety-split, down the hill with the mother bear hot on their trail. I stood stock still, and she raced right past me. Ha, she thought I was a stump.

There was no time to slide or scramble down the bank, so the men decided to both take a flying leap into the icy river. That didn't deter the mother bear, and she plunged over the edge right after them.

Perhaps the icy water cooled her temper, or maybe she decided that as long as they were swimming they were no threat to her cubs, but for whatever reason, she left good enough alone and decided to return to her cubs.

By the time she scrambled out of the water, back up the bank, and lumbered back for her cubs, I was long gone.

Shortly after I got back into falling after my accident, Eddie Crombie contacted me to see if I'd be interested in falling for the WAC Bennett Dam project, north of Prince George. He was foreman for Carrier Lumber Co. who carried the contract to salvage as much saleable timber as possible above the rising water of the new Williston Lake. I didn't hesitate. I had known Eddie some years earlier when he was a teenager. Quick and wiry, practical and even-tempered, he was a pleasure to work under. Carrier Lumber was reliable and paid good wages. I gladly spent six adventure-packed years working for them, while the Dam Project continued. I held the record for the longest-lasting faller for the company.

The sawmill and main camp were at Finlay Forks, along with a small store and fuel tanks. The Parsnip, Finlay, and Peace Rivers converged here before the lake came to be, but my work took me anywhere up to sixty or seventy miles across the lake and up either the Finlay or Parsnip Rivers. My job was to cut, top, and limb as many trees as I could. Much of this was virgin timber—beautiful, big trees.

Transportation was by riverboat in summer and by Skidoo in winter, both with their own set of challenges.

My riverboat was a low, sturdy structure, thirty-six feet long, with a 35-horsepower motor, well able to ride out a stormy lake or swift currents. But because the water was rising up to sixty feet per year, I had to be on the lookout for floating and submerged debris and logs. Tops of trees poked through the surface of the lake, or they were hidden below. It helped to have a spotter up in the bow. (My brother, Frank, worked with me part of the time. Leander would come and limb and top for me during school breaks, and sometimes I hired Indian help.)

This man-made lake is now the biggest in BC, with about 8,000 miles of shoreline. While I was working, the shoreline was constantly changing, not only because of the rising water but also because of major landslides. Mountainsides or large sections of bank just slid into the lake, causing a fair-sized wave, let me tell you. I didn't pitch my tent on shores or hillsides in summer. It was much safer and very handy to build a raft for my tent. In many places, the shores were so lined with debris one couldn't land. Moose are excellent swimmers, but I saw more than one moose drowned because it could not fight its way through the tangle to shore after crossing the lake. That was something I hated to see.

One night, I was snug in my bed in my tent, when I woke up to a tipping raft and splashing sounds. Seemed like some big visitor was making a call. Sure enough, in the moonlight I saw a determined moose trying to clamber aboard, but my little raft was about to capsize. I had to put an end to that.

After killing the moose, I promptly skinned and quartered it. The Indian ladies would be happy for the hide and the meat.

That night I got another animal visitor, but this one worked so quietly it didn't even wake me, or Frank, up. That was one quiet bear. We woke up to find only one quarter of the moose and its hide left. If that robber got a stomachache, it served him right!

For short runs to and from work each day, I kept a handy aluminum boat. One morning, I loaded a couple chainsaws, mixed gas, lunch bucket, and various wedges and tools and set off about seven miles to where I was falling for the day. I liked to get an early start so I could quit early and get back to camp in time to make a nice supper, maybe with a fresh caught fish, tune my saw, sharpen the chain, and study my Sabbath School lesson.

At the work site, I tied the boat securely to a stump and set off with my number-one saw, leaving the spare saw, oil, and lunch in the boat.

The terrain was steep, but I put down a lot of trees before stopping for lunch. Looking forward to my sandwiches, I headed down the hill. But where was my boat? No boat, just a gas can, a few things floating around, and about three feet of the butt end of a fallen tree sticking out of the water about where the boat should have been.

There I was in the wilderness with no boat! One of the trees I had fallen had plummeted down the hill in direct line with my boat, pushing it down into the water, along with the motor and whatever else was on board that couldn't float.

Sending a quick SOS heavenward, I found a long stick and fished in my lunch bucket, gas can, and whatever else was floating, while deciding what to do. I had to try to retrieve my boat.

I pulled up on the butt end of the offending tree. It actually rose a little. I peered down into the water. It was very clear, but I could see nothing.

I pulled more and more—five feet, eight feet. Ah, something shiny showed up far below.

I sawed off a chunk from the butt and kept pulling. Cut and pull, cut and pull. I kept repeating this until the boat was twelve or thirteen feet from the surface. I could see the outboard was still attached, but the boat had snagged onto a lot of old debris plus some standing treetops. It was caught fast. I tried this way and that to free it, but I couldn't budge it further.

Now what? The water was icy cold, and a boat trapped under twelve feet of water didn't look like any picnic. Besides, I was alone. I couldn't walk back to camp. I could make a raft, but it would take all night to get to my tent and then some.

I must attempt the twelve-foot dive and try to free the boat from that tangle of trees and branches. If I took off my clothes, I could get dry and warm after getting out of the water. I dove in and reached the boat. Hanging on to the rascal tree to keep me stable, I grabbed the boat with my other hand and started pulling. I got another hold, and pulled some more, hanging on to the tree to keep me down. It was coming inch by inch. How I hated to leave that boat, but I had to surface twice for air before I finally freed it.

I cheerfully baled out the water, cleaned the water out of the outboard, and dried off the spark plugs. Now for the test. A few pulls on the cord, and the motor sputtered to life.

I was home in time to make supper.

Winter travel with the Skidoo was faster if I wasn't pulling a heavily loaded skimmer and Skiboose. My machine had a 25-horsepower motor, the fastest available at the time, and it could step out lively.

Not too far from the Forks was a mountain known for its fine jade. A woman mined the jade, getting around with her own helicopter.

She landed on the ice right close to our place one Sunday. Being a gentleman, I stepped out of our trailer and asked if she'd like a ride up to Budd's. Budd ran a small grocery store out of his trailer.

"I'd appreciate a lift," she said.

But this was no ordinary lady. She was a pilot and a miner, someone who was obviously ready for adventure. I didn't want to disappoint her. All I had was a 25-horsepower Skidoo, but I made the most of it on the ride to Budd's.

As she got off, she commented, "Hmm, quite a ride! Could I return the favor?"

I politely declined.

When the guys heard about it later, one of them said, "What? You refused an offer like that?"

"I'm not that crazy," I said. "After the ride I gave her!"

Winter travel on the lake was treacherous. As the lake bottom settled, sometimes bubbles formed. As the bubbles streamed up, they would actually melt the ice, and within a few hours, thick ice could become eight feet of open water. Another hazard was that the water level might drop several feet, leaving a big airspace between ice and water. Also, the ice surface had plenty of buckles and ridges, not always easily seen, white on white.

Talking about ridges . . . I was home for the weekend at Finlay Forks, and I asked the family if they'd like to go for a Sunday drive. I wanted to take a drum of gas to camp with the pickup. We spent a pleasant time together, when I hit the king of ridges. We heard and felt a tremendous BUMP behind us.

"Check that barrel, Leander," I said. "Is it still on?"

He turned and looked. "Yep. Still standing."

Imagine our surprise when we reached the camp and went to unload the barrel to find it upside-down.

Of course, in winter my tent was pitched on land. You might be surprised at how comfortable a tent can be in the dead of winter—much warmer and drier than the men had in the trailer bunkhouses at the main camp. The trailer bunkhouses featured ice half way up the walls and no circulation to dry clothes at night.

I pitched the tent inside a larger plastic-covered enclosure. Near the tent sat my tin stove. I could come home, get a good fire going, change my clothes, and have everything dry by morning.

Sometimes the wolves sounded pretty close, but they never bothered us.

We would see them on the ice quite often, checking the wooded areas where the trees stuck through the ice. The moose loved to browse the tender treetops, but they would sometimes break through if the water level had dropped. The ice would form cones around the trees, but moose just don't have enough intelligence to figure out unfamiliar dangers, and so they were the victims too many times.

Frank and I were falling timber on the ice one time over water about twenty or thirty feet deep. Even with that much of the tree under water, there was still a lot of tree above ice, for this was virgin forest. Although logging trucks were used on the lake in winter, most of the logs would be rounded up and taken to the sawmill in summer after the ice was gone.

I couldn't hear Frank's saw, so I decided to work closer just to make safety checks a little easier, for the ice here was known for its treacherous thin spots.

As I made my way toward him—I could just now hear his saw—my feet broke through the ice. I flung myself forward on my face, and the saw and I both slid to safety.

Frank later returned to the hole and measured it. There were three feet between ice and water. I would not likely have gotten out. The angel of the Lord was with me again. I think I kept him pretty busy.

On another occasion, I lost my chainsaw through the ice in about twenty feet of water. A saw is worth a lot to me, so I found a long stick and prayed that I could get hold of the saw. I fished and I fished until I felt something solid. Was it just a rock, or . . .? The stick had a little hook on the end of it, but it would have to hook on to the handle of the saw to work, and of course I could not see a thing.

Yes, it hooked onto something. I started to carefully draw it upwards. It was coming. At about fifteen feet, I could see the saw—up, up, almost to the top, barely on the hook . . . just a little farther. Then I had it in my hands.

"Thank you, Lord."

I cleaned the water out of it and went back to work.

The Wolverine

I spotted the creature as soon as it came onto the ice. Even that far off, its strange lope and plumed tail gave it away.

"A wolverine!" I gave a low whistle. It was heading for a clump of half-submerged trees sticking out of the ice near the middle of the lake.

Wolverines are the largest cousins in the weasel family and are notorious for their fierceness and cunning. In all my years of trapping, I had never caught a wolverine. At times they stole from my traps, sometimes even taking the bait without springing the trap, leaving only their big footprints to tell the story.

Indians and trappers had told me stories of wolverines actually hiding traps or lifting latches to enter and rob cabins. Whether or not those stories were true, I thought, "Here's my chance to get me a wolverine."

Finlay Forks Adventures

A wolverine pelt was worth a hundred dollars. It is rare and beautiful fur, prized for its trait of remaining frost-free (making it superb for lining parka hoods). For mounting, the value went even higher.

I stopped and got my rifle ready, and then I cut him off from shore. He headed for the trees. I was pulling a skimmer (a toboggan-like sled) and a Skiboose, together carrying about 1,800 pounds, to set up a new camp about sixty-five miles from the Forks, so I just took my time. I smiled to myself. He's mine. When I get close, he'll run up a tree, and I'll have him, I thought. There didn't appear to be any other options.

I stopped a little ways back from the trees. They were sticking out of the ice about twenty-five feet, and the wolverine had literally vanished in them. Aware that this thirty-five pound dynamo can ambush and bring down a caribou or moose and will even challenge a bear or cougar, I checked my 30.30 before heading cautiously for the trees.

Every time I took a step, I heard a low growl, but I couldn't see his head sticking out anywhere. I continued to take a step at a time, alert for any movement. I stayed on the side he had entered to head him off if he made a dash for shore. I was a little afraid that if he came out he'd come straight for me.

But where were those growls coming from? As I got closer, the mystery was solved. I could see that the water had frozen onto the trees, and then the water level dropped, leaving chunks of ice hanging onto the trees, including handy holes around the base for him to climb into.

Hmm! How would I get him out even if I did shoot him. This me-stepping and him-growling was a useless game. Better try a different strategy. Maybe if I just went back to the Skidoo and kept very still and quiet, he'd come out of seclusion.

I sat and waited for a whole hour. It didn't work.

Never Say Whoa In A Bad Place

Then I had another idea. I could put a little gas down the hole and throw in a match. That would bring him out , but where would he go? Probably straight for me, fighting mad. And if I weren't quick enough, what then?

I had a long way to go and a camp to set up before dark. I decided that I would rather be a live chicken than a dead duck.

During spring thaw and fall freeze, lake and river transport pretty much came to a halt. Fortunately, these two seasons are usually short and fast in the North.

One spring, break-up came so fast between weekends that there was water already on the ice.

"We'll just sit here and wait a couple of days for Eddie to come and airlift us," I told my two hired hands. "I'll have to come with the riverboat for the Skidoo and the rest of our equipment as soon I can get in."

"But I have to get out NOW," one of the Indians told me.

"It can't be so urgent that you're willing to risk your life for a two-day wait," I told him

"I have to get to town. I can't wait two days."

I tried my best to reason with him, but no sirree. He wasn't listening. After hours of listening to his grousing, I told him, "Get on the Skidoo! You're going!"

We set off down the river and across the lake. All of a sudden, I saw a stretch of black water, about twelve feet across. The ice was wet and slick. There was no chance to stop or turn. You know the saying, never say whoa . . .

I opened the throttle wide and hit the water at full speed. The spray shot out everywhere, but we made it across.

I looked back to check on my passenger. He was dripping wet, but he never said a word.

Grizzly

"Do you see that little lake down to the right? I landed there a couple weeks back to check out an abandoned camp—tent, gear, boat, and all. I've inquired around about it. People say it's been there for over a year, and it'll be under water soon," Eddie said. "You need a motor for your riverboat. There's an Evinrude Thirty-five—just what you need. It would be worth your effort to hike in there and pack it out with whatever else you can carry. What do you think?" He turned his plane so I could take a better look.

We were flying over the Finlay end of Williston Lake, about sixty miles from the Forks, scouting for a new area for me to fall. He circled the area to check out the feasibility of this side project. The small lake was about two miles off the main lake on the other side of a low ridge of dense growth. In a matter of months, it would become part of the larger reservoir as the rising water took over.

We could see that it was wild country, a great place for moose, wolves, and bear. The shore of Williston was lined with an ugly two hundred yard border of debris, deadheads, and floating logs that would have to be crossed by foot from wherever I docked. The whole setup made me a little uncomfortable.

"Pardon me for saying so, but I'm not ready to try it alone. How about joining me some Sunday."

"Sure thing," he agreed, and he headed the plane back to Finlay Forks.

A few weeks slipped by. The days were getting shorter. I woke up early one Sunday with the feeling that there'd never be a better time if I wanted to get that motor. I rolled out of bed and hiked over to Eddie's trailer.

"Yep, I'm willing," he said.

I headed back home and got pancakes going for the family. Before breakfast, as usual, we shared a Scripture text and prayer. I chose one of my favorites. Psalm 34:7 says, "The angel of the Lord encampeth round about them that fear him, and delivereth them."

After breakfast, I grabbed my packsack, a blazing axe, and the lunch Jean had prepared for me. Eddie was waiting for me by the lake. We set off across the lake in his speedboat.

It was a beautiful day. Eddie drove while I sat in the bow to spot deadheads in the shimmering water.

Around eleven o'clock, we figured we should be getting close to our destination. He slowed down and found a place to tie up the boat. We ate part of the lunch and left the rest in the boat for our return. I shouldered my empty pack and slipped the single-bitted, short-handled axe into my belt. Eddie also carried a pack and a 22-caliber pistol in a holster under his shirt.

We gingerly but quickly stepped from log to log, reaching shore safely. Ahead of us, we had about a two-mile stint through the brush. We hit on a pretty good animal trail, so I didn't need to blaze as much trail as I expected. We figured we should be back to the boat before five. That still gave us four hours before sundown, as twilight lingers long in northern summers.

Arriving at the abandoned campsite without incident, we found the remains of a complete camp: some rails from which hung pieces of rotting canvass (the tent), cooking utensils, tools, grub box with some canned food, a rat-chewed bed-roll, and by the lake, a wooden boat with its outboard motor still attached.

Eddie rummaged through the tent-site, loading his sack with tools and utensils, as many as he felt he could carry. I unbolted the motor from the boat and tied it to my packsack in as comfortable a way as possible to carry.

We were both anxious to get going, and we didn't waste time at the site.

As I said, the country was very brushy. As we headed back, Eddie commented, "There sure are a lot of signs of moose around here."

"Yes," I said. "But not only moose. I can smell bear."

I barely got those words out of my mouth when we heard the cracking and crashing of some large animal approaching us from the left. Did I say approaching? Charging would have been a better word.

Eddie was about ten feet ahead of me. I don't know what he was thinking, but I imagined that within seconds we would be facing a charging cow moose.

I called, "Here she comes, Eddie!"

The next instant, with a tremendous roar that seemed to shake the very ground we were standing on, a giant grizzly blasted out from the undergrowth right in front of Eddie. I can still see its blood-red mouth open wide, lips snarled, and fangs bared as it bore down on us.

We were trapped. It is unthinkable that a man can outrun a bear even under more favorable conditions. But we were in dense scrub pine loaded with heavy packs.

"Eddie, stand your ground!" I shouted, thinking of past experiences with bear.

The monster charged straight for Eddie, leaving no doubt to his intent. I dropped the pack from my shoulder as I ran toward the grizzly, shouting at the top of my lungs, waving my arms, and banging on a gas can. That took him by surprise. He hadn't noticed that there were two of us to deal with. Without breaking stride, he veered away from us and circled counter-clockwise.

I returned to my pack, hoping he would understand that we had no intention of threatening him. But, no, that bear had one bad attitude. He simply gathered speed for his second attack. I feverishly worked my axe from the pack. Eddie dropped his heavy pack. Everything was happening at lightning speed with no time to plan.

"Eddie, hold your ground," I cried again as the maddened grizzly came after him again. For the second time, I ran at him, hollering and flailing my arms. Why he veered off again I couldn't tell, but he was so close I could feel his breath on my face.

As the bear retreated for the second time, so did I. Again he circled. Eddie and I both managed to free our weapons before he made his third furious charge.

I hollered and raised my axe. I was going to bring it down across his nose with all my might, for his nose was his vulnerable spot.

With a louder roar and wider mouth, he came for us again. Eddie's pistol looked pretty small, but if he could just shoot into that wide-open mouth . . .

The grizzly swerved but not before brushing me with his hip—he was that close! Neither of us got the opportunity we needed. I didn't dare hit him anywhere but on his nose, knowing that if I missed, I would infuriate him worse.

I couldn't believe that we had been charged three times and were still alive and unhurt. This time our attacker retreated only about ten yards. Our stalling tactics had bought us about as much time as we were going to get. Swiftly it swung and loudly it roared as it plunged full speed toward us.

"Shoot, Eddie, shoot!" I hollered. Its wide mouth made a perfect target, and it was probably the only place a little 22 could effect serious damage.

BANG went the gun. Down went the bear. But the bullet had only hit his chest. Wounded and madder than ever, he rolled on the ground, tearing up young trees and sending clods of dirt sailing over our heads. Fur flew as he clawed at his chest.

This was the break we needed. I took off running for the biggest tree in the area—a birch only about ten inches in diameter, tall, smooth, and essentially branchless for the first fifty feet. I slipped up that birch like I was sliding downhill, with Eddie right behind me. Looking around, our attacker sighted us (we weren't exactly camouflaged) and lumbered our way to investigate.

We shimmied up a bit higher, to about thirty feet. My axe lay at the foot of our birch, but Eddie still had his pistol. Our biggest fear now was that the bear would literally pull this perch of ours right out of the ground. We didn't doubt that he could if he so chose.

"Maybe aim for his eyes," I said.

But the grizzly seemed to change his mind. He stopped behind a screen of willows and sat there swinging his arms at us. What a fantastic specimen he was— his giant head was a good eight feet off the ground.

We waited for him to come out of his hiding place so Eddie could get a good shot at him, but he just sat there threatening us. And so began the waiting game—we the prisoners, clinging for our lives to the trunk of the slippery birch, and the grizzly, our guard, resting behind the willows, nursing his wounded chest.

Our muscles began to ache and cramp. Minutes seemed like hours. Almost one and a half hours later, he was still just watching and waiting—no urgency now.

Finally, Eddie said, "I've got to go down. My arms are cramping so bad."

As he began to slide, I clung even tighter to the trunk with one arm and grabbed Eddie's shirt with the other, pleading, "Come on, Eddie. You can do it. That bear will kill you if you go down now. Try to get a shot at his head. It's so big you can't miss."

So what if he couldn't hit a vital spot. The grizzly was too far to do much damage to anyhow, about fifty feet away behind those bushes.

Something had to give.

In desperation, with all the concentration he could muster, Eddie took aim through an opening in the willows. The shot rang out, and the grizzly toppled right over on his side. His feet kicked back and forth, then all was still. Could it be possible?

Eddie started to slide again.

"Not yet. Hang on a little longer. I'm afraid . . ."

Just at that moment, the bear gave another kick, got on his feet, and headed our way.

Oh, no! What now? Was he going to topple our refuge and bring us crashing to the ground? Or would we simply lose our grip and drop down for him? Eddie had one shot left. The prospects held us to the tree like superhuman glue.

The giant slowly circled our tree and looked up at us, kind of dazed-like. The two bullets had apparently had some effect. Eddie muttered to himself, "Should I let go my final shot?"

As if in answer to his question, the bear turned and sauntered down the very trail we needed to take.

Every few steps, he stopped, turned, and rose on his hind legs to check if we were staying put. We obliged.

Seconds after he disappeared, we slid as quietly as possible down the tree. But we had no assurance that our nightmare was over. Maybe the bear was circling around and would attack us again. Perhaps it was lying in wait. If our tree had had a few good branches, we would have gladly roosted in them all night.

While stretching out the cramps in our arms and legs and getting some circulation going again, we decided to head for our boat. Yes, it meant following the trail of the bear, but we couldn't come up with a better alternative. Leaving our heavy packs so we wouldn't be encumbered, I picked up my axe and followed Eddie who was cautiously moving down the trail, pistol cocked, stepping, looking, listening in the fading light for any indication of the presence of the king of the forest whose domain we were trespassing.

After an hour or so with no sign of the bear, I began to relax. As I relaxed, I began to shake. Finding our boat in the dusk presented quite a challenge of its own. We had to leave the trail at the blaze and head down through dense brush to the shore, guess the whereabouts of the boat, and strike off across the driftwood over twenty feet of water, hoping our boat was waiting for us at the end of our two hundred yard obstacle course.

As I stepped from log to log in the waning twilight, our Scripture text of the morning kept repeating in my mind: "The angel of the Lord encampeth round about them that fear him, and delivereth them. The angel of the Lord encampeth round about them . . ."

I said to Eddie. "Our guardian angel sure was working to protect us from that grizzly, or he would've had us."

He answered seriously with gun still in hand, "We aren't in the boat yet!" And he wasn't trying to be funny.

Did it ever feel good to step into that speedboat! Heading into the blackness of a shore-less, log-strewn lake at night was a picnic compared to the previous few hours.

A few weeks later, I was again scouting with Eddie in his plane. Below us, crossing a swamp, was a big grizzly.

I jokingly said, "Here's your chance to get even."

He turned the plane so quickly, I was sorry I had said anything. He zoomed down toward the bear.

The grizzly stood up on his hind legs, swinging his arms at us. There was no cover for him to run to. We decided that was enough to even the score.

A few weeks later, Eddie and I returned for the outboard motor and our packs. We scouted around and found an old moose kill. Obviously, the grizzly felt he was defending his food supply.

It sure would have helped if we could have communicated with him a little better. I guess that's true for most fights.

Chapter Twenty-Four

Little Horn Ranch

It was in 1972 that I got a most unusual invitation from Hazel, my brother Lewis' wife. She had bought a cattle ranch up near Tatla Lake and wondered if I would manage it. About 250 miles west of Williams Lake, Tatla Lake is beautiful wilderness ranching country. It would be like stepping backwards in time maybe fifty years.

Fireworks followed.

"No way are we going on some wild goose chase! Count me out!" Jean said in that no maybe tone.

"Look at it this way, Dear," I pleaded. "The older three are already gone, and we have only a few more years before Leander and Jewel are grown and gone. What an experience for them. They'd never forget it! And I could be more a part of their lives again."

Did I see some softening? I pressed my advantage. "Why not give it a try for one year?"

It would be stretching it to say Jean agreed with enthusiasm, but she agreed.

Little Horn Ranch was in a postcard setting about halfway between Tatla and Tatlayoko Lakes, with the snowcapped coastal range just to the west. The main gravel road ran alongside the valley, cutting between our ranch layout and the hay meadow, which ran north and south for about a mile, with a creek meandering through the middle of it. That far north we only got one crop off a year, about 800 bales, enough for eighty to one hundred head of cattle. The interesting thing about our hay meadow was that the better part of it was on top of a lake, on a two-foot thick mat of peat. In places, the ground moved if you jumped. If you poked a twenty-foot board through that layer, it was in water. We had to drive the tractor slowly to keep down ground swells! (A good part of our summer was spent in haying.)

Little Horn was a small ranch, and it came with a less than desirable reputation throughout the valley. I had a little cleaning up to do, but the neighbors were hospitable people—helpful and loyal. The Schuk Ranch was next to ours; it was home to wonderful people. Some folks didn't get out to Williams Lake more than once a year, so if anyone was going to town, they let us all know so they could pick up things for the rest of us. Even the mail from Tatla Lake was dropped off to all the neighbors along the way back by anyone who made it out.

In summer, we ran our cattle with the Bracewells' cows up on the Potato Mountain Range, named after a type of wild potato that grows up there. Potato Mountain doesn't look like rangeland. The lower parts are heavily treed and brushy, and above that, all you can see from the valley are high, rugged peaks, but behind and between all this are lush meadows.

The Bracewells ran about 300 head, and they hired a full-time cowboy for the full season, June 15 to September 15 (from the end of bear-hunting season to the beginning of deer-hunting.)

We had to load and truck our cattle twenty miles to the staging area, where there were holding corrals for branding, vaccinating, and castrating before the cattle were turned out to range for the summer. Of course, I took my turn riding the range. I had brought Chief to the ranch, and he loved riding in the mountains.

Lee (Leander) and I rode out one cold, bleak day to check the cattle. Winter was setting in early. Coming through a stand of poplars, we saw a cow moose. To add a little interest for Lee, I suggested, "Let's catch her."

Just a nudge was all the encouragement Chief needed. He took off in hot pursuit.

The moose galloped along the bank of a small river in her ungainly gait, but I could see that my horse had a distinct speed advantage over her. At this point, the moose decided to change her tactic by taking a sharp turn to cross the frozen river. Wrong choice. All four feet went out from under her, and splayed flat, she slid clear across the ice. Picking herself up on the other side, she indignantly trotted off.

Even Chief had a grin as we turned back to our task.

Fall was a busy time since we had to round the cows off the hills before the winter storms hit. We fed the cattle through the winter, and early spring was busy with calving. As soon as the snow had melted off the hills, the cattle were put out on the range, but the work was not over. We regularly rode the range, checking on the cows, watching for bears, and searching for strays.

I was riding Chief on Potato Mountain above Tatlayoko one day, when I heard a Chip! Chip! Chip! behind me. I turned to see what was making such a fuss.

A little chipmunk was racing after us as if he was a cougar. It was almost comical—almost, because believe it or not, he literally attacked us! Yes, he raced right up Chief's back leg!

"What's this?" I said, and gave Chief his rein. He wasted no time, and the chipmunk fell off. I stopped Chief and looked back at the chipmunk.

Poor little thing. It was skinny, eyes bulging, fur bristled, and panting. Maybe I should catch it and take it in to be checked for rabies, for he certainly wasn't behaving like a normal chipmunk.

I dismounted and took a step toward it. It jumped at me, and down came my foot in defense. No more chipmunk.

So, I can say I've been attacked by a grizzly AND a chipmunk!

With summer came welcome visitors to the ranch.

Renee, one of Jean's nieces, came with her Labrador to spend a couple weeks with us. I don't think she was all that impressed with the looks of Kyla, our Catahoula. At least, we got that impression, because we heard quite a bit about the skill and training of her fine Lab. (Catahoulas are an American breed of dog raised for ranching, herding, and hunting. They are strong, broad chested, have a dominant personality, and weigh anywhere from sixty to eighty pounds. Kyla had the leopard markings, blue eyes, and intelligence for which they are famous.)

Renee joined right in with the tasks on the ranch. Being a true lover of horses, she enjoyed the riding best of all. We were starting to take the cows down off the higher mountains before any freak snowstorms hit, and Renee was right there, along with the dogs.

Suddenly, the dogs started barking, and we could tell they were giving chase.

"Aha! Sounds like they found a bear," I said. "Let's check them out."

Sure enough, by the time we got there, the bear was treed—matter of fact, about forty feet up! Kyla and the Lab were both looking up expectantly.

BANG! My gun went off. Kyla jumped back quickly while the Lab continued looking up into the tree, almost grinning.

WHUMP! Down came the bear right behind the Lab. You should have seen him take off for home. I could almost hear him thinking, Whew! That was quite a bird!

Well, Little Horn Ranch was a venture we won't forget. The little school didn't have a whole lot to offer the older students, but I don't think Lee and Jewel regretted the venture. And we forged a number of friendships with several ranching families in the area who joined us for Bible study and fellowship. (We didn't learn till several years later that one of these couples actually made their decision to follow the Lord and were baptized!)

Meanwhile, Hazel's daughter, Marcia, and her husband were ready to manage the ranch. Jean breathed a sigh of relief as we returned to the regular world, which for me meant the bush.

We had to leave Chief at the ranch for a few years. As soon as circumstances allowed, I brought him home. He looked pretty rough, but he responded well to a little extra care and attention. I was soon riding him again.

One day, as I entered the corral, Chief greeted me with his usual nicker as he came to meet me. I rubbed him down a bit and started puttering around in the corral. Chief returned to the manger. Suddenly, he leaped straight up in the air, and fell on his side. I dropped what I was doing and ran to him. He looked at me apologetically, and it was game over.

I have warned many a starry-eyed young horse-lover to never get too attached to any one horse—a hard lesson I suddenly discovered I hadn't learned too well.

Chapter Twenty-Five

Coastal Adventures

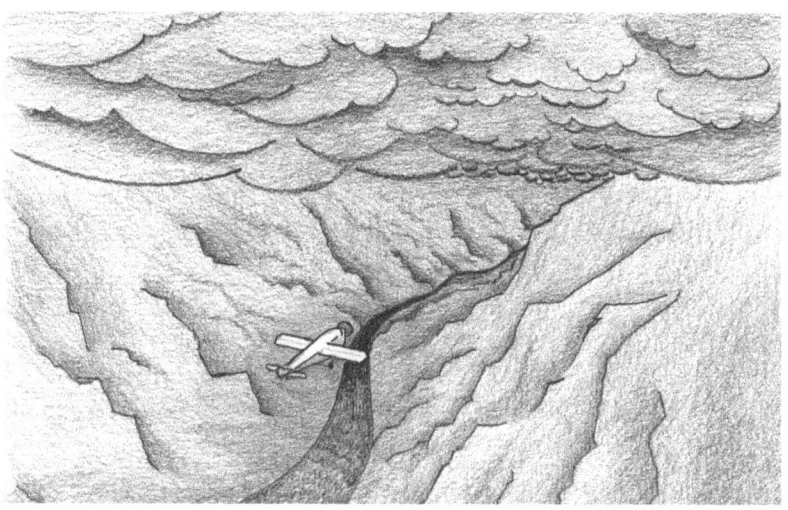

Back to the world of logging, I soon got a job with Steve Crombie, who was working around Lilloet. Lee was sixteen, and he wanted to get a job too. He was a natural with machinery, so he was hired on as a skidder—a very daring job with the steep terrain we worked on. But with higher risk comes better pay, and he soon was purchasing his own skidder. Why go back to school when you can make that kind of money? (He skidded until after he and his wife started a family. Then he decided the oil fields in Alberta were a safer bet, and he did very well as a cat operator there.)

I usually worked at falling, but I filled in as needed. One day Steve asked me to take the new skidder down to the landing. It was a 404

Timberjack three-speed automatic—the latest and biggest for its time.

"Sure thing!"

Steve either had a lot of confidence in me or else a strange sense of humor, for no one gave me any instructions on how to run the thing. I started it up, and everything went fine until the first corner. It was a sharp one, so I took my foot off the accelerator.

Oops! I'm in big trouble. The steering has gone out on this thing.

Over the bank I went and down the mountainside, trees going by on the left and on the right! A big fir was coming straight for me.

Well, if I'm going to hit her, I might as well hit her good, I decided. I stepped on the accelerator.

Hey, what's this? The steering is working just fine again.

I missed the tree, but it sure could have saved me a heap of adrenaline if I'd have known that the steering and the accelerator worked together before I started down the hill

Steve joined with his brother Frank and moved their logging operation to the coast. It was a long hike from our home in Silver Creek, near Salmon Arm. Fortunately, Steve had a small plane and Leon, a brave young pilot, to shuttle us back and forth for weekends. Fog and high mountains are the order of the day along the coast, and Leon flew through thick or thin. Following the Fraser River canyon, he would sometimes fly in the canyon to stay below the fog. It gets pretty narrow in places—I was glad it wasn't my responsibility to keep the wings from touching either canyon wall.

We were heading up the coast past Squamish in pea-soup fog one day.

"I'm going to fly above this stuff," Leon said, and soon we were up where the sun was brightly shining.

We flew and flew, expecting to get past the clouds and fog below, but there wasn't a break. We began to wonder where we were. Had we passed the island? Were we flying out to sea? Our fuel was getting low as we peered down, trying to get a glimpse of the ground below to get our bearings.

Suddenly, there it was—but it was gone just as quickly. Leon circled back to check it out again—a clear, narrow funnel through the clouds with welcome-looking ground below. Did we dare risk trying to descend through the funnel?

Leon figured the alternative was no better, and I had already checked my standing with the Lord. Down we went in as tight a spiral as I ever care to fly.

Oops! Lost it—found it—made it through! Thank the Lord! Leon recognized the area immediately, and we were soon safe and sound at camp.

Faye Crombie was our camp cook. Young and able, Faye really earned her paycheck. Besides cooking breakfasts and suppers for the crew and washing dishes and pots and pans, she baked fresh bread every evening to make into sandwiches early the next morning.

Sometimes I would poke my head in the cookhouse door to see if I could give a hand with the dishes.

One evening, Faye was sitting by a table weeping as if her heart would break. I stepped inside, and I immediately saw her batch of fallen bread even before she poured out her tale of woe to me.

"I can't face starting a whole new batch," she said, and the tears started again.

"You know my Catahoula has more pups than she can handle," I started.

Faye looked up. Yes, Kyla had twelve pups, but what did that have to do with her problem? I could almost hear her thoughts.

"I've been thinking they're ready to start on some solid food," I continued. "Dry your eyes and make me a deal. Let me have your bread for my pups, and I'll trade it for a fresh batch of dough. I'll mix some up quicker 'en a cat can blink her eye!"

I was already tying a tea towel around my waist. I formed another one into a baker's hat. Faye couldn't help but grin, and she was soon scurrying around getting the ingredients I needed.

My experience as a baker came in right handy that night.

It was high time for me to hang up my helmet and retire from falling, but I had forest fever pretty bad. I quit for the winter several times before I made my final break in my early seventies.

Even as a full-time horse trainer, I keep my chainsaws tuned up and filed ship-shape—one just never knows.

Chapter Twenty-Six

Retreaded

I had been falling trees for Steve Crombie, one of Eddie's brothers, pretty steady for about ten years. But I was getting more and more requests to help people with problem horses. My Sundays were kept busy.

Like I've always said, "There's more than one way to skin a cat," and everyone's got his own ideas of how to train horses. Always on the lookout for better ways to do things, I read books by several trainers. Then videos started coming out—Roberts, Shrake, Pirelli. I picked up pointers from here and there and worked them into my style.

I was almost seventy before I decided I wasn't going to wade through knee-deep snow with my power-saw anymore. It was time to retire. Horses and firewood kept me pleasantly busy all winter. Spring rolled around and I got a call from Steve.

"Hey, John. Do I ever need a good faller."

I fell for it and was off again.

I retired several times the next few years—every winter, in fact, while the requests to train horses continued to come more and more. One day I was finally ready to pack in my saw for good (except to cut rails and firewood) and turn more of my attention to horse training.

Jean had always enjoyed being outdoors and doing things, but she felt something amiss with her energy. She checked in with her doctor, and after many tests, we were told she had leukemia.

For Jean, chemotherapy was out of the question. As a family, we promised to respect and support her decision. She read up on natural remedies, and our pastor and elders had a special anointing service, praying that God would answer as He saw best.

She remained amazingly positive, with ups and downs, but no pain, mainly just a decreasing amount of energy.

One morning after a rough night, she said, "John, I think it's time to take me to the hospital." I took her to the hospital and called the family and told them that I thought they should come.

She was gone before evening.

As hard as it was to lose Jean, it was a comfort to know it was not by choice. It is also comforting to know that we will be reunited if I remain faithful to the Lord.

For the next few months, I had a health problem of my own that I needed to attend to. A German herbalist and a special diet took care of the problem. During this time, I also did some traveling and visiting with my children.

As the months passed, I was amazed at how lonely I was. I went from day to day, seeming to function, but not really all there, even though I kept myself very busy, so busy that I sometimes lost track of time.

One morning, I told myself, "This is a good day to get firewood for Sister Ritchie."

I loaded my saw, wedges and axe, and gas and oil into the back of my pickup and trundled off down the road, past the church . . . what was going on at the church? Several cars and trucks were parked outside.

I glanced at my watch. It was almost nine o'clock. Suddenly, it dawned on me. Today is Sabbath!

I hustled home, got changed, and hurried back in time for song service.

After Jean's funeral, I had emphatically told my family I would not even consider a third marriage—two are enough for any man! However, as the months passed, I truly began to wonder.

July rolled around, and I made plans to attend the BC Camp Meeting at Hope. It is always such a wonderful time to see family and friends and enjoy a spiritual feast. So I headed down with my little camper trailer as usual. Now I could understand why my brother Lewis had complained that a widower doesn't stand a chance. Plain and simple, we're outnumbered. But I bumped into a friend of Jean's from Grandview Flats days—Peggy.

The more I thought about it, the better the idea seemed. However, before getting involved, I ran the possibility past my kids. I phoned each one to ask permission to pursue the friendship. Do you think that's silly? It is a switch for a parent to ask permission from his kids to date, but I was not going to risk losing my family at this stage of life.

They all knew Peggy and had gone to school with her kids. All five of them told me to go for it, so I did.

Peggy and I have had thirteen years together. In fact, I owe most of those years to her, for shortly after our wedding, I had a strange fainting spell at a Goertzen reunion. She made me see my doctor as soon as we got home.

"You've got the heart of a young man. It's not your heart," the doctor assured me after some tests. "Maybe it was the heat or not enough water, or your low blood pressure."

I was a little embarrassed for even bothering him.

Strangely, a few months later, for no apparent reason, I just keeled over again. Under protest, I visited the doctor again. He diagnosed the problem as a bundle block, and he installed a pacemaker that would kick in if my heart stopped again. Shortly after, my heart stopped beating on its own permanently.

Although Peggy was not a rider, she appreciated and supported my interest in horses. My everyday tools were now ropes and halters, rings, straps and clips, boards, and fences and gates.

I enjoyed the challenge of my job, including the fact that the horses that got as far as me had already figured it out that they had the edge over these two-legged weaklings. My first job was to win the horses' trust, then their submission. Depending on how they had been handled, this took anywhere from two days to two weeks.

Next, they needed to be bitted, reined, and driven using ropes and rings in what I call a "W." This was all done from the ground before I ever got into the saddle.

I remember two fine Arab mares, a dark sorrel and a pinto. Both were registered horses. They had been spoiled, and the owner was actually afraid of them. I could see why, especially of the sorrel. Her name was Knasha, but I nicknamed her Jezebel. She was nasty. I would walk into her corral, and she would immediately lay back her ears and turn her heels to me. I worked on that, and within two weeks, she was following me around like a puppy. But every step of the way started with a fight.

"I think I've found more than my match," I said several times, wondering if I would have to admit defeat.

But by the time my granddaughter Melinda came for Easter break to help me, Knasha was ready for riding. (Melinda would ride the green horses, and I would ride my trainer horse, Gypsy.) We rode many miles, through the river, over bridges, in the hills, past flapping plastic, and on the busy road. I had to know that Knasha knew exactly where her feet belonged.

I worked on those two horses almost three months. Finally, I phoned the owner to let him know his horses were ready and that he would need to spend some time with me so they'd all be working off the same page.

He came out, but you could feel the bad blood between them.

"I just don't trust those gals," he said. "In fact, I'm scared of them, and they know it. I owe you quite a bit for the training. How about me giving you the horses and their papers for what I owe you."

Talk about a deal! I passed it on to my two granddaughters who were living northeast of Grand Prairie, Alberta. They rode those horses for three years before selling them to help pay for college.

Chapter Twenty-Seven

Gypsy

Of all the horses I've owned or trained, I never met a smarter horse than Gypsy, my last riding horse.

My friend, Burkhart, approached me one day and said, "John, I'd like a dependable, well-trained horse that I could use. Would you help me?"

That was an invitation I couldn't pass up.

"Sure. Why not start with the auction sale coming up in Armstrong?" I suggested. "If you know what you're looking for, you can sometimes pick up an excellent horse for a good price."

We got there early to look things over. A rancher from Alberta arrived with a truckload of horses. I watched as he was unloading.

Gypsy

"There's our horse." I pointed her out to Burkhart. "See her confirmation. Look at the way she moves and behaves with the other horses. She's got good horse sense."

We got a chance to talk briefly with the rancher. "Yeah. She's an excellent calf-roping horse, a real worker," he told us.

Color-wise, she didn't really have it. She was kind of a red roan-almost-appaloosa mix. We bought her for five hundred dollars.

Actually, she was more horse than what Burkhart had in mind, so after he got a fine colt from her, he gave me first dibs on her.

I thought, Why not? I can always turn around and get my money back and then some.

But you know, the more I used her, the less I wanted to sell her. She became my number one horse. Gypsy was agile. She could step backwards over a log, slide down a steep bank on her rump with a rider on her back, and turn on a dime and give change on a nickel.

And she was smart! I've always figured the average horse has the reasoning capacity of a three-year-old, some maybe up to four or five. But Gypsy must have been a horse Einstein. She became my effective partner, nudging, nickering, nipping, or modeling. If I got a bitey, kicky, disrespectful colt, I could just put him in a corral with Gypsy, and after a day or two of being bossed around, told when to eat or not eat, when to move, where to move, how to move, he was one grateful, cooperative colt when I was ready to lead him out of that corral!

She definitely expected to be number one in pecking order, next to me. I was amazed how loyal and cooperative she was when she realized I was boss. Even then, when she was unhappy about where I wanted to go, she would change her usual smooth gait to a rough, choppy one, just to let me know what she thought about it.

Like many horses, she enjoyed being chased. If children wanted to ride her, she would take off across the pasture, tail in the air, as if to say, "Catch me if you can." She'd wait till they caught up to her, then repeat the performance. When she played hard to get with me, I would just sit down in the field. She would circle around and around in tighter circles until I could touch her foot. As soon as I touched her, she'd stand still. I'd keep my hand on her, stand up, pull the rope from my pocket, and shake it out while she waited quietly.

However, she was not always like this. When Gypsy first came to me, she couldn't seem to stand still. Her feet were moving even when I said, "Whoa." This bothered me, so I set out to change that habit. Maybe that's when she decided I was truly the boss. She learned not only to stand still but even how to turn around while keeping either her front feet or hind feet in place.

Gypsy enjoyed trail riding. Sometimes a friend would bring his horse trailer so we could go up in the hills to ride. As soon as Gypsy heard the trailer come into the yard, she would whinny her recognition. I'd open the corral, toss her reins over her neck, and she would trot up the hill and right into the open trailer.

I mentioned that Gypsy was agile and very quick—an important trait for any good cutting horse. Once, at a gymkhana, I thought I'd like her to join a race. Thinking that an eighty-year-old like me might not be up to it, I looked around for an aspiring young rider.

"Would you like to ride Gypsy?" I asked a young fellow. "You'll need to be able to hang on, 'cuz she flies like a bullet."

His eyes lit up. "Oh, could I?"

Before he was even in the saddle, she knew he was an inexperienced rider. At the start signal, she set off sedately, returning with her rider safe and sound, but far from first place.

An annual highlight since retirement is Cowboy Camp meeting, an event that allows a group of thirty or so riders to meet, ride, and

Gypsy

fellowship together for a few days. In 1989 we met at the Reiswig Ranch above Falkland. It is beautiful country. One can see Highway 97 far below, with traffic scurrying like so many ants, the meadows of Douglas Lake Ranch, and Kamloops City off in the distance. I was legally blind by this time, so I could only see it in my memory, for I was familiar with the area.

Our group consisted of riders from Kelowna, Silver Hills, and even Vancouver Island. Sabbath afternoon we took a long trail ride. On the return trip, I took up the rear to encourage those who were lagging behind and to be available to help with any problem horses. One lady was having trouble with a borrowed horse, so I offered to trade mounts for an hour. After settling down her horse and switching back to Gypsy, she hurried on to catch up with the group. I had been so occupied with her horse that I wasn't sure if there were any riders still behind me, so I waited a while to be sure before carrying on.

As we passed a gate, Gypsy seemed determined to turn in. I wouldn't give her her head, but I thought her behavior was quite out of character for her. Because of my macular degeneration and disorientation from working with the problem horse, I did not realize that we were already at the place to turn in.

We continued on for a while until the road ended. I realized then that we had overshot our turn, and that the gate where Gypsy had wanted to turn was indeed the right one. Now what? It was late afternoon. I could pretty much judge where the camp was. If we cut across country, we could be there before dark.

We set out. It was rough, steep country. We came to a deep valley with heavy brush and marshland and crossed a creek. I figured that just up the other side we should be back to a road, but something was just ahead of us. A high, sturdy five-wire drift fence blocked our path.

It was too rough and too late to retrace our steps. I did not have the tools to take down the wires. In my younger years, I would have just camped out overnight, but I knew this old body just wouldn't take the drop in temperature.

My mind was whirling. Would she? Could she? With serious misgivings, I dismounted, clicked my tongue, and motioned for her to jump. It was taking a terrible risk—both our lives depended on that jump.

Her muscles bunched, and over she went with inches to spare! If her master figured she could jump that fence, then she must be able to—it was just as simple as that.

I climbed over the fence and back in the saddle. As the toe of my boot slipped into the stirrup, it hit me. The two things that Gypsy had demonstrated—total trust and submission—are exactly what God wants from us.

Gypsy clambered up the hill and onto the road I was expecting to find. Just a couple of gates to go and we'd be home. It was dark and she was in a hurry. She had covered a lot of miles that day.

I continued riding in the hills around home between the Salmon River Valley and Enderby for seven years, after becoming legally blind, something I could never have done without a dependable horse like Gypsy.

I needed a new riding pad, so Peggy took me by a tack shop in Enderby. The fellow was watching a training video—sounded like Richard Shrake. I asked some questions about it, and the fellow responded that he was going to use Shrake's method to halter-break his colt, Joe. We exchanged a little chit-chat, I wished him good luck, and I went on my way.

A couple of days later, I stopped by to pick up the riding pad.

"How are things going with Joe?" I asked, always interested in horse news.

"Not too well," he admitted honestly. "There are a few things I'm just not sure about."

His frank openness appealed to me.

"You know, there's many ways to skin a cat, but if you'd like me to show you a few tricks of the trade, I'd be happy to give you a hand. You'd need to pick me up, because I'm legally blind and can't drive."

That was the beginning of a very special friendship. We shared a mutual interest, and we hit it off from the word GO. He'd come by every few weeks and take me up to his ranch, or we would go look at stallions or other horses, or whatever.

I knew the time was ripe for me to give up Gypsy. Van had a quiet, steady way with horses. I couldn't think of anyone who deserved her more. She took to Van very well. I would not be at all jealous if he took first place in her life now, but I notice that when I visit the ranch, she still comes and stands next to me.

Van raises racehorses, thoroughbreds, below the Enderby cliffs. He has a set-up of fenced pastures, corrals, and stables. Gypsy was a natural mother and was very protective of all the foals. She would not allow any stray dogs in the pasture. Van figures that if the cougar that lurks in the fifty-foot cliffs near his ranch ever tried to attack a foal, Gypsy would probably fight him off. I figure he's not far wrong, from the five-claw rake she sports on her rump. She was ornery enough to shake off one cat and would probably do it again if she had to.

One time, she alerted Van with a sharp scream. He checked to see what was wrong, and he discovered one of his mares tightly wedged in between a hay wagon and a barbed-wire fence. He ran for the wire cutters and saved the mare. Meanwhile, the foal discovered she was cut off from her mother. She panicked, and tried to run through the fence. Gypsy ran around two gates and through three fields and led the foal safely to her mother.

Van says she runs the show on the ranch. If a foal pulls rank, she straightens him out. She stops horses from cribbing (chewing on wood—bad for the fence and the horse) and puts the mares into the night corral, including herself. She then holds them till Van closes the gate.

No one saw what triggered this next event. Perhaps Gypsy was just looking for attention, but one day she gave chase to two geldings. She galloped them around a two-acre field two or three times before getting them into a corner. They were so desperate to escape that they crashed right through the fence. They both got up and went to stand on the road, probably wondering what to do next.

Gypsy knew she had done something wrong, so she ran up to the window of the house where Van was and whinnied very loud. He looked out, saw the two geldings, and ran to grab a couple of halters. Before he even got outside, Gypsy had run back across the field, out through the broken boards, and herded both geldings back into the field. She stood there, holding them, while Van got a board and some nails to fix the damage.

One spring Van asked me, "Would you like to help me trailer some thoroughbreds to Maple Grove Ranch for breeding? I've got sixty warmbloods from Washington, California, Alberta, and Saskatchewan—lots of them high-caliber racehorses. I'm thinking of breeding Gypsy, too."

Sounded like an interesting day coming up. "Sure thing!"

When Van unloaded Gypsy, the breed rancher said, "Put her in that field with them mares over there."

I could tell Van figured it wasn't the best idea, but he quietly did what he was told. I thought, Oh oh! Here comes the show.

Almost immediately, Gypsy noticed two of her mares were in the herd. Her ears and tail went up as she approached the herd. Two or three hierarchy mares stopped her in front of the herd to challenge her. Down went her ears and tail, and she screamed, running backwards and kicking wild. Everyone was scared. The other lead mares melted back into the herd, and she ran them until she cut her two mares out from the rest. She did a little victory dance and then stood alone between the two herds. What a girl!

Only two days later, Van called to say that Gypsy had just broken a record. She was already bred and Mr. Ditloff was almost begging him to "get her out of here!" (Breeders like to keep your mares for anywhere up to two weeks. Every day puts another ten dollars in their pocket.)

We had a good laugh about that. Yes, Gypsy's quite a horse. I wonder what she'll do next.

This was his last story. Since then, on May 4, 2001, Gypsy had a beautiful little cowboy filly with a blaze and little socks with freckles on them.

PART III:
FAMILY MAN

Conclusion

You may wonder why this man with a big family has so little to say about them. He enjoyed telling stories, but he was too wise to brag about us and too loyal to tell on us. We knew he would not betray us. We were safe!

We also felt safe with Dad because he never lost his cool—either his temper or his presence of mind. Like with most kids, Dad was our hero. In fact, he was the hero of almost any kid that knew him, and even of many who were no longer kids. He wasn't our hero just because of the neat things he could do or the amazing life he had led, he had a way of making a person feel special. He honored others.

Yes, we respected him, but he respected us. Even when he had to punish us, it was done fairly, quietly, and privately. He believed in us, encouraged us, and let us try our wings.

So, we, his children, want to finish this book by sharing personal stories of our dad, unfading memories, lessons never forgotten—stories of an ordinary man with extraordinary common sense who never said whoa in a bad place.

Never Say Whoa In A Bad Place

One of his granddaughters wrote the following:

He had a way about a horse
That was as strong as it was mild.
With patience and great understanding
And an unerring sense of timing. . .
And he called it "common sense."

He had a way about a child
That was as strong as it was mild.
He didn't have to say a lot,
The lesson never was forgot. . .
And he called it, "common sense."

He had a way about his God
That was as strong as it was mild.
Breathed its essence all around,
A sermon heard without a sound. . .
And he called it "common sense."

by Melinda (Pond) Hindley
December 2000

Chapter Twenty-Eight

There for Me

Contributed by Donalda (Goertzen) Jones

It's difficult for me to find an early memory without Daddy in it—he was always there for me. His unconditional love is my picture of God.

Just shortly after he married our new mom, he took us all to Stanley Park in Vancouver for a day. On our pony ride, he led Marilyn's pony so she wouldn't be afraid. We rode a miniature train and had a picnic. It was all so grand.

When we moved to Stay Falls, he built a bedroom cabin. Kenneth had the first part, Marilyn and I shared a part with bunk beds that he hung from the wall, and off our room was his and Mommy's room. I can still smell that fresh, new-lumber scent and remember how he made everything we did seem like such fun.

The little sawmill nearby had an open wooden flume with a belt that carried the sawdust out to a pile. Kenneth discovered it and showed Marilyn and me how to climb out on the flume and jump off the end into the sawdust pile. Daddy wasn't afraid to let us explore and experiment . . . to a point.

After a cougar had been spotted in the area, Daddy warned us not to wander too far away. Kenneth and I decided to visit an old abandoned mill site. We had so much fun that we forgot about the time until it started getting dark. We knew that we had better hurry home. And it was then that we remembered about the cougar.

Just then, who should we see coming to meet us but Daddy. Boy, were we glad to see him, until we noticed the absence of his usual smile. That was one of the few times his belt came off, teaching us that it's not good to disobey.

After the tears were dried, we safely walked hand in hand the rest of the way home.

During that first year at Stay Falls, we three children went to spend a few days with our first mother. When she took us home, I decided I was going back with her. I put on quite a show.

Dad calmly said, "Children, why don't we go for a walk?"

That sounded pretty tempting, but I still hesitated.

Turning to Kenneth and Marilyn, he held out his hands and said, "Let's go see what we can find on the trail."

They started off without me. That just wouldn't do. I was not about to be left behind, so I ran to catch up. (My nickname, Me-Too, wasn't without a reason, nor did Daddy need a degree in child psychology to figure out what made a child tick.)

There for Me

Oh, how my knee hurt! I went to show Daddy.

Sure enough, it looked red and puffy. Daddy took out his trusty jackknife.

"Here, let me have a look at it," he said.

I held very still and tried not to cry as he carefully tried to remove the sliver. He could tell it was very big, but this was one time his jackknife just couldn't do it. So we headed to the doctor.

The doctor was surprised at how big and hard and white it was, and he checked to make sure it wasn't a bone splinter. Apparently, I must have landed on a stick, and it broke off inside my knee.

At Kitwanga, Daddy was away a lot, but he still found time to do neat things for us. He made us an awesome merry-go-round with a couple of wagon wheels and a teeter-totter board. Kenneth could get it going fast enough that I got the breath knocked out of me a couple of times when I fell off.

The hill behind our house was steep enough that Daddy decided to make us a ski hill. He cut down a wide swath of poplars and bush. It made a wonderful run for our sled, toboggan, and shared pair of skis.

One day he came home with beautiful, warm Indian sweaters for each of us kids. It was one of his trades with a native family who wanted a set of books but couldn't pay cash.

One weekend, as we passed the sawmill on our road, Daddy turned to make sure he had our attention. "Children, I do not want you to play in that sawdust pile anymore. They are burning it, and it takes a long, long time. Even though you can't see any fire, it's burning big caves underneath that you could fall into." He went on to tell us about a team of big horses who had broken through and been burned to death. He repeated, "Don't ever go near that sawdust pile." (He knew that was Marilyn's and my favorite spot to play.)

Weeks went by. Marilyn and I got out of school one hour ahead of Kenneth, and as we passed the sawdust pile, it looked inviting, except for the black, burned area around the edge. We hadn't seen any flame or smoke for a long time. Surely it was safe by now.

We agreed to stop and play for just a little while. Marilyn chose a place near the edge. Being a little more adventurous, I scrambled up farther till I found a nice, clean hollow. I grabbed a slab for a bench and jumped into the hollow. Through the crust I dropped, letting out a whoosh of steam from below. I managed to hang on to my slab with one hand, and with the help of my guardian angel, for sure, I was able to pull myself back out.

Marilyn had come to visit me. She stood frozen to the spot.

Two frightened girls hurried home. My right foot hurt so badly, so I stopped to take off my boot. It was full of hot sawdust. I shook out the sawdust and removed my stocking. Immediately, a blister started to form, so I quickly put my stocking and boot back on and hurried along as best I could.

Mommy scolded us when she met us at the door, but almost immediately she noticed many small blisters on my face. With horror, she watched as I tearfully removed my boot and stocking to reveal my foot.

She had no car or phone, and I wouldn't let her touch it. By the time Daddy came home, gangrene had set in. The smell was nasty, and red streaks were going up my leg.

Daddy carried me downstairs, and amid my screams, started hot and cold bath treatments that he strongly believed in. The first few dips were hard, but then my leg became numb, and he continued the treatments into the early morning hours—hot water from the boiling kettle, and icy water from the creek.

Daddy stayed home till the streaking was gone and the proud flesh disappeared. But it was several months before I was able to go back to school.

When Kenneth was tragically killed at Babine Lake, he took Marilyn and me to the cabin where he had prepared the body for burial. He gently explained how our brother was sleeping till Jesus comes to wake him up. What an example of love and faith he set for us!

Much of our childhood was spent in the woods. Daddy taught us what to do if we got lost, how to keep track of direction, and what berries to eat and which ones to avoid. I never saw a person who could walk so fast and lightly in the bush and see so much. Certain seasons, he would come home with his hardhat full of mushrooms. Fried up, they sure tasted yummy, although I was afraid one day I might get a poisonous one. He was no stranger to cooking, and with the help of his trusty pressure cooker, he could have a tasty stew ready in no time.

I was about nine, and we were living up north at Progress when I got dreadfully sick. After days of vomiting and fever, with every joint in my body aching, Daddy wondered if I might have polio.

With a basin for me to throw up in, he laid me on the backseat and headed for Dawson Creek to see a doctor. We had to wait several hours to see the doctor, so Daddy decided to buy some ginger-ale and see if that would ease things a bit. I took a few sips, and that's all it took. I was better!

Sagebrush tea was another of his home remedies. It tasted terrible, but he said it was good for the stomach and the blood.

A cold compress under a scratchy wool sock was a must for sore throats, and it seemed to work. Anything Daddy did was fine with me—I thought he could walk on water if he chose to.

Mom was not one to enjoy Christmas, perhaps because it was a tough time of year financially. But Daddy would remain chipper. He'd reach into his pocket, get a look of surprise on his face, and say, "Look what I just found! Let's go to town."

There'd be a small wad of dollar bills in his hand, and off we'd go, each with maybe one dollar to do our Christmas shopping. But it was fun!

My favorite memories of Daddy are horseback riding with him. He always taught me something neat. We'd sing songs and share thoughts that we wouldn't do anywhere else.

When I made foolish choices, he never threw it in my face. Even when others thought I'd gone over the brink, he let me know that he had faith in me, and he told me how special I was to him. What a dad!

Chapter Twenty-Nine

Through the Wilderness

Contributed by Marilyn (Goertzen) Pond

I was three when Daddy came to pick up Kenneth, Donalda, and me from Manitoba. Mrs. Giesbrecht and Mrs. Reimar (his cousins) and their families had been caring for us. The long train ride back to BC is my earliest memory. Daddy gave us new coloring books and crayons, and at night, our seats became bunks. Donalda and I slept on the top bunk, and we could peek down and see Daddy and Kenneth. When Daddy went to the washroom, we managed a short pillow fight. It was exciting and even a little scary to walk from car to car. The parts between the cars were very noisy, and the metal floor moved strangely where the two parts met. I hung tightly on to Daddy's hand.

We ate some meals in the diner. One item on the menu was scrambled eggs. They must have been very good for me to remember them this many years! Aside from the terrifying toilet that was ready to swallow me up—when you flushed it, the little metal disc at the bottom tipped, and you could see the ties flying by below—it was a wonderful trip. The most special part was being with Daddy.

Spankings were rare, and the memory of them even rarer. Daddy believed that form of punishment was best before memory kicked in. I remember only two, and I'll share the first one. (I was four.)

The big people were visiting at Grandma's on a beautiful Sabbath afternoon.

Kenneth asked, "Daddy, can we go for a walk with Ron?" (our cousin)

"Sure, but don't go too far. Stay close enough so I can call you," he said, thinking of the high river out past the pasture.

Off we went, first down to the pond at the bottom of the hill. We checked it out for frogs and snakes (both on our good list). Then we went on up through Aunt Hilda's strawberry patch to the cow pasture. We could spend hours there. Our chief entertainment was turning over dry cow pies to see how many shiny beetles, centipedes, and other wildlife we could uncover. After they all scurried away into hiding, we'd go on to the next one. Of course, we visited the red salt block and chipped off a small piece for each of us to lick.

We eventually worked our way into the woods that skirted the pasture. Ron and Kenneth broke off some long willow branches to wave in fancy maneuvers, when suddenly we heard Daddy calling. We realized we had been gone too long and too far, and we dashed toward the voice, hoping to make up for lost time. We met him at the top end of the strawberry patch.

"I've been hunting and calling for a long time. Do I have to help you remember your promise?" He started removing his belt as he explained how important it is to obey.

Since he started with the oldest, I figured I might have time to run to the house. Surely he would forget me by the time it was my turn. Oops! It didn't work.

"Marilyn!"

I turned and went back.

Our wedding was a huge event in our life. We now had a mommy, and we could live at home. A few months later, as we children were discussing our wedding, it led to whom we would marry when we grew up. I knew without a doubt, I was marrying Daddy, and all Kenneth's reasoning couldn't change my mind.

About this time we moved to Stay Falls, near Mission. The damp, coastal climate caused my arms and legs to ache so badly that I sometimes couldn't sleep at night. Daddy was a light sleeper, and if he heard me quietly crying into my pillow, he'd come with his horse liniment and rub my limbs till they would numb up.

Moving days were fun for us kids, and we had lots of them—moving days and kids, particularly when Aunt Naomi's three children joined us. We'd take turns, two at a time, riding in the loaded truck with Daddy. He'd point out interesting things to see, teach us how to recognize different trees, or tell us neat stories about the olden days. But best of all, this was the time for special music, solos sung especially for us—his favorite was "My Lord knows the way through the wilderness, all I need to do is to follow." He also sang funny old songs, like "Roll 'Em, Girlies, Roll 'Em," and "Big Rock Candy Mountain," or old cowboy songs. He would even yodel for us. Wow!

When we didn't live up in the bush (Canadian for woods) with him, he would batch and come home for weekends. Donalda and I knew of no better vacation than to spend a week in the bush with Daddy. Our job was to keep the floor swept, carry in the water, and fix potatoes for supper. Other than that, the day was ours to explore, cut out paper dolls from the catalog, and make houses in the woods.

Daddy would get up early and start the fire while Donalda and I snuggled in the warm sleeping bag on the homemade bunk. Sometimes it was pancakes for breakfast—full-sized flapjacks, flipped campfire style. Other times, it was porridge—not my favorite, but definitely better cooked on Daddy's airtight heater—and making toast was a work of art. He could toss a slice of bread against the side of the hot airtight and it would stick there till toasted, then drop off automatically. (So what if we picked it up off the floor.)

One evening he brought home a big lump of beautiful clear amber pitch. He cleaned out a can and announced that we were going to try our hand at making gum. He melted it down with sugar, but it was pretty bitter. We added more sugar and some vanilla. Donalda chewed it, but I figured it wasn't one of his better experiments.

One time I had a big, cracked, nasty wart on the top of my right hand.

"Let's get rid of that thing," he said, rummaging through his shelves. "If we could cut the air off from it, it couldn't live, could it?"

He found some rubbery red airplane glue and painted it on quite generously. Believe it or not, my wart was gone in no time, never to return.

Returning to the cabin early, one day, he simply said, "Come. I have something to show you."

We hurried through the woods after him to where he had been falling. He motioned for us to slow down. We picked our way over some logs, and he said quietly, "Watch your step!"

There, right in front of us, lay a tiny fawn, so camouflaged on the forest floor that we hadn't even noticed it. We could have touched its nose, we were so close, but it didn't so much as flick an ear.

At another camp above Lavington, between Vernon and Lumby, he was sharing a cabin with Ezra Hirschkorn, so he set up a tent for our week's vacation. At night we kept hearing a high-pitched whistle coming from the steep, rocky mountainside.

"Those are rock-rabbits," Daddy explained. "They are also called conies or pikas. They live in colonies, usually above the tree line. Come and see how they prepare for winter."

We climbed up the rocks and peeked into their little caves at their tidy little haystacks stored for winter.

Daddy made a box-trap to catch one alive so we could observe it up close. It was grayish-brown with a light-colored tummy and a short bunny-like tail and short round ears. Although it was full-grown, it was tiny—about six or seven inches.

This same camp had another interesting feature on the other side of the road—a cave big enough to walk in. Being on the north side of the mountain, there was still ice in it, and the men used it for their fridge.

After cleaning up dishes one morning, we thought it would be nice to make something special for supper. What did we have to work with? We went through the shelves and found a box of Jell-O. Now, that was a rare treat indeed. With the help of the cave, we would surprise the men with dessert tonight.

"One cup boiling water, one cup cold water," we read on the back of the box. Washing dishes had used up our hot water, and we had already let the fire go out for the day. Actually, since the Jell-O had to cool down anyways to thicken, wouldn't it just speed the process if we used two cups cold water to begin with? It made sense to us, and we quickly set to work, stirring it well. Then out to the cave with it—such anticipation!

We checked it a few hours later. Too soon; we had plenty of time yet.

However, it was still runny at noon.

By four o'clock, we knew there'd be no Jell-O for supper. Rather than waste it, we decided to divvy it up between us, taking turns with a spoon.

Taking the bowl of liquid to our tent, we sat on our spruce-bow bed and took turns. About half way through, Donalda noticed something strange in her spoon. We bent to take a closer look—a WORM! A little green worm. Oh, no, it was HALF a worm!

We looked in the bowl. The other half wasn't there. Donalda figured I got it, but actually, the chances were pretty good that she got it. Anyhow, we decided to ditch the rest of our Jell-O juice.

We were pretty quiet during supper, and we slipped back to our tent as quickly as we could. A little later, Daddy came and asked if he could come in.

"Yes."

He made a little small talk, and then asked, "By the way, did you see a box of Jell-O on the shelf?"

We told him the whole story, and how sorry we were that we had ruined the surprise. He smiled and said, "You know, I wouldn't bother about it at all, but it wasn't my Jell-O."

Oh, no. This was even worse than we had thought. We apologized to Mr. Hirschkorn, who, being a father himself, was very understanding. We never knew how Dad discovered the missing Jell-O so quickly. He was probably relieved that we hadn't planned to sneak it but disappointed that we tried to hide our mistake. But instead of scolding or sermonizing, he showed us how much better it is to own up.

By word and example, he taught us to appreciate nature—a fawn, a rock rabbit, a flying squirrel, a mother quail and her fluffy brood, or a glen purple with lady slippers. Sometimes it felt like we were standing on holy ground. Even after I was grown and married, he took Doug and me out in the wilderness to show us some nesting Canada geese near 100-Mile House.

He had a way of making us feel special, often in just little, everyday ways: a warm hand on the knee of a restless four or five year old in church, a special smile that said I knew you could!, asking his teenagers what our plans were, respecting our decisions, and offering cautions or a helping hand if we bombed out.

A special memory often repeated through my teen years was coming home. Donalda and I went to Canadian Union College for tenth grade. I was fourteen. It was just months after his worst logging accident, and we were dirt poor. Somehow, come December, he scraped up enough money to send us a train ticket to come home for Christmas. No matter what the weather was, or what time of night it was, or how far he had to come, or what the road conditions were, he was there waiting for us. After a warm welcome, he carried our luggage to the old pickup and gallantly opened the passenger door for us.

Years later, in his eighties, legally blind, and living in an apartment block, Dad always waited outside his door to welcome us, and he saw us out to our vehicle. He was showing us honor.

Never Say Whoa In A Bad Place

In October 2000, Mom Peggy was looking forward to her granddaughter Krista's wedding in California. Dad had been diagnosed with cancer a few months earlier, and he didn't have the energy for the trip, so Donalda and I arranged to go and stay with him. Lee and his wife Jennifer had arrived a few days earlier to pick up Banner, a beautiful young gelding they had bought from Dad. We had a marvelous time reminiscing, gallivanting around the country, and checking on Gypsy. Christine, our almost sister, joined us for half a day, and Jewel and her family joined us for Sabbath. We decided to have an old-fashioned home Sabbath School for her girls.

Some thoughtful Goertzen cousins, hearing that we were planning to be up there and feeling that there might not be four Goertzen brothers left by next summer, hastily planned a family reunion at Vernon for Sunday. It was so much fun seeing Dad and uncles Frank, Lewis, and Clarence enjoying themselves, looking through old picture albums, recounting the long ago, and playing Crokinole. Those guys were mean shots at Crokinole—even Dad with his poor eyesight.

On the way home, Dad commented, "I felt so honored to have you there!" (This was a humbling lesson for me on honor. How many reunions had I missed because I was too busy?)

A month later, I was back in Salmon Arm. We had had a hectic summer, and Doug could not seem to find a good time for a vacation. The year would soon be over, and he would forfeit two weeks of vacation time if he didn't use it by the end of the year. So, better late than never. Doug knew my dislike of cold weather and was trying to come up with suggestions of how to pleasantly fill my time.

"No need to worry about me," I told him. "I'm just going to sit down with Dad for two weeks and have him tell me his stories while I jot down notes. You can putter around on our cabin."

And that's exactly what I did. How we enjoyed ourselves. We

Through the Wilderness

talked and laughed and cried through his stories. Interestingly, when I told him what I came to do, Dad said, "I want to start with the story of Gypsy, the smartest horse I ever had." (Maybe because he figured I had heard all his other ones already.) We got a good start.

Vacation time was over. We reached home Friday afternoon. About 1:00 a.m. the phone rang. It was Mom Peggy saying that Dad had had a stroke and was in the emergency room. We quickly threw a few things back into the suitcase, arranged for someone else to preach the next day, and headed back.

Dad lived another three weeks. His mind was clear, and he responded with his eyes and one hand, but he never spoke again. (How thankful I was for our delayed vacation!) He acknowledged each of his guests—and there were many of them. We had no idea how many had borrowed this man as their dad or grandpa!

I could see Dad's disappointment when I told him the doctor could not stop his pacemaker. He had requested earlier that he not be kept on life support in a terminal situation, and to him, that pacemaker, with about six months of battery-life left in it, fit that category. He loved life, but he was not afraid to let it go.

For two weeks he was given water through IV's. During the final week, we were almost all there with him. We sang and told stories during the day, but nights were harder. We took shifts watching over him.

On Christmas Eve, Donalda, Frank, Doug, and I were on till one. His breathing was labored, and I felt that this was the night. I didn't want to leave, but our shift was over in fifteen minutes. I asked to pray.

We held hands. My prayer was short and simple, "Lord, please let Daddy go to sleep . . . soon." I stopped and opened my eyes to regain control. Wondering if I was finished, the others opened their eyes too, just in time for us to see Dad's eyes open as he took three little breaths, and was gone.

Donalda closed one eye, I closed the other, and I finished my prayer, "Thank you, Lord!"

Donalda's nursing instinct led her to put her hand on his chest, and her eyes opened wide. "It stopped," she gasped. "His pacemaker stopped!"

"My Lord knows the way through the wilderness, All I have to do is to follow . . ." I can hear my Dad sing.

Chapter Thirty

Calm Amidst Storm

Contributed by Christine (Poulson) Cross

Uncle John was more like a father than an uncle for my brothers and me. I was six when I realized that Uncle John meant what he said, and that he did not expect to repeat himself. We were living in a big old log house, and I was fooling around on the stairs, trying to stick my head through the rails. Uncle John was working on his saw below and noticed what I was doing.

"Christine, don't put your head through the rails," he warned.

I did it anyway, and would you know it, I got stuck. No matter which way I tried, I could not pull back my head. That in itself was terrifying enough, but even worse was the fact that I had disobeyed. I knew what I deserved, and I screamed as only I could scream!

Uncle John came bounding up the stairs, turned my head just right, and drew it out. Then, instead of the spanking I expected, he gave me a big hug and said quietly, "I thought I TOLD you."

Uncle John's Chief was the most beautiful horse I had ever set eyes on, and I was sure my life would be forever complete if I could just ride him. I figured I had plenty of experience in riding to handle a well-mannered stallion like Chief.

"Can I please try?" I begged.

Uncle John got Chief saddled and ready; then he handed me the reins and gave me one brief instruction, "Don't let him run."

I gave the horse a little kick—first mistake. He took off like a shot. I grabbed for mane . . . saddle . . . anything, screaming my head off—second and third mistakes.

Somehow I stayed on as he turned and galloped full tilt for home. As he thundered up the road, Uncle John stepped out directly in front of him.

"Whoa, boy!" he said firmly.

Chief came to a stop and put his muzzle into Uncle John's hand. Talk about my hero!

But what I appreciate most was his faith in me. Even when I did foolish things, he never judged or criticized. When my own mother couldn't be bothered to attend, Uncle John proudly walked me down the aisle on my wedding day.

Chapter Thirty-One

The Rescue

Contributed by Bonnie (Goertzen) Johnson

Dad was a cheerful person who liked to see us happy, but that didn't mean he didn't expect to be obeyed. He meant what he said, no ifs, buts, or maybes.

I was about ten when Dad was sheep ranching along Chase Creek. I wanted to go horseback riding with Neil, but Dad told me I needed to do my chores first.

I still can hardly believe what I did next. I got so angry that I flung the oat can as hard as I could at him, turned, and ran for all I was worth.

Never Say Whoa In A Bad Place

In a few bounds, he had me, and I got exactly what I deserved!

As he held me afterwards, he said, "Bonnie, I did not spank you because you have a temper, but because you lost your temper. I want you to remember, temper is not a bad thing, it's what you do with it that matters."

I've always remembered that lesson.

I could tell many stories about my dad, but I have chosen what I think is the most extravagant one of all. Dad's sense of responsibility to his children went far beyond the call of duty, and it included his grandchildren.

The year was 1986 just shortly after Mom passed away. My life was going badly. For extreme reasons, I felt it was in the best interest of my two youngest children to move away from me. I allowed their father's brother to take them to Prince George until things settled down. (Since I don't feel comfortable about using his name, I'll just call him Brock.) When I felt it was safe, I got my brother, Lee, to drive me from Camrose, Alberta, to retrieve them. They were only two and three years old.

When we arrived at the trailer, Brock met us at the door. "They're not here," he told us insolently. "Come in and look for yourselves."

The children were gone, and Brock had no intention of giving them back. I was devastated! Because of my bad choices, I believed I had lost my children for good. I had already moved Triena and Rod to my sister's in Spirit River for their safety. My emotional stability went from bad to worse.

Through it all, Dad never once stopped believing in me.

We knew that taking the children by force was not an option. The legal system told me I had no recourse, because the children were with relatives to whom I had entrusted their care. I could take the uncle and

The Rescue

father to court and gain an interim custody battle, but I did not believe I had the emotional or financial strength to win such a battle. I was defeated!

Dad phoned me and with deep emotion said, "They're our babies, and we are going to get them back! That man is up to no good for them."

He knew how fragile my state of mind was, and he spoke reassuringly of the plan he and Lee had devised. He ended with, "It's going to be a fight, and we can do it. But we need you to come along."

Dad drove Doug and Marilyn's Bronco up to Spirit River pulling a horse trailer. He took a route through Prince George, where he met Lee and me.

Lee and I got to Prince George before Dad, so we drove by the trailer court where the children were supposed to be. To avoid the chance of being detected, we didn't get too close. There were no signs of the children, except for some small clothes on the clothesline.

We drove back to town and met Dad at the designated place. I joined Dad, and Lee headed back to Alberta. Dad was calm and self-assured. It gave me courage. "First, we apply for a custody hearing," he told me as we drove to the courthouse.

The hearing was set for the following day. We had no choice but to wait. Instead of sitting and wringing our hands in some hotel room, Dad found a place to park the horse trailer, and then we drove to the trailer court. The Bronco was an unknown vehicle, so we drove closer, but there were still no signs of the children. He backed off across the road and parked in some brush where we could watch.

We noted the time Brock came home from work. But there was still no sign of the children. What if he had gotten wind of what we were doing? Would I ever see my babies again?

"I have an idea," Dad said. "They don't know who I am. Why

don't I take a walk?"

He got out and walked along the road while I held my breath. Brock had a reputation of violence. Was I jeopardizing our lives and maybe the lives of my babies?

Dad casually walked through the trailer court and back again at a leisurely pace, smiling and nodding at the people he met. He slipped into the brush and then the Bronco, and he gave me a big smile. "Our babies are there. I heard David crying."

I was never so glad that David cried. We wanted to barge in, grab them, and run, but we had to go slowly and by the law. We sat there and watched the trailer until the lights were all turned off; then Dad started the Bronco, eased out of the brush, and headed back to the hotel. We caught a few fitful hours of sleep.

In the morning, we dressed carefully, grabbed a bite to eat, and headed back to the courthouse. I think we were the first ones there. We didn't know when our case would come up, but we weren't taking any chances!

As we waited, we prayed that we would not have to wait long and that the judge would rule in our favor. (We wanted to be long gone by the time Brock got home from work.)

We were third on the docket. We were told that the uncle had already begun proceedings for permanent custody based on the allegation that I was an unfit mother.

Dad quietly but firmly told the judge that we were not leaving without a court order to remove the children from that home and that the children's safety was at stake.

Fortunately for us, Brock's name was not new to the judge. He was known to have guns and to be a troublemaker. Because of the allegation against me, we could only get an interim judgment, but that was enough.

The Rescue

We were out of there by one o'clock. We had three hours to pick up the horse trailer, rescue the children and get a head start on Brock. We were sure he would pursue us.

Because of the man's unsavory reputation, Dad suggested we enlist the help of the RCMP. We drove straight to their station, and they dispatched an officer to recover the children. We followed behind the police car to the trailer park. He parked right by the step, while we parked out on the street. Questions were racing through my mind: Were the children there, or had they been moved again? After all these months of waiting, would I be disappointed again?

The officer walked up to the door and knocked. No answer. He knocked again. I think I must have been holding my breath. Dad reached over and squeezed my hand.

The door opened and the officer stepped inside. The door closed. Dad stepped out of the Bronco and waited. My heart was pounding so hard I'm sure it was making my blouse vibrate. It was hard to sit there, but the officer had asked me to stay inside the vehicle.

The door began to open, but no one appeared right away. The lump in my throat felt so huge that I was sure I could never swallow again. Just as I thought I couldn't handle the suspense any longer, the burly officer stepped out onto the porch with a child in each arm. I jumped out and ran to meet them.

Lori looked at me somberly, but David was laughing and crying at the same time. Both children reached out, and the officer placed them both in my arms. They smelled of urine, but who cared!

David turned to the husky officer and said, "Thank you, Mr. Policeman, for finding my mommy."

Turning to me, his little face wet with tears, he said, "We were babysatted for a long time, and we ate all our moose meat!"

We got into the vehicle while the officer talked to Dad. He had found the children locked in a back bedroom with a padlocked slab gate. The girlfriend told him she could not open it until the children's uncle returned.

"I'll have to cut the lock," he told her. It was then that she produced the key.

"I'd have the children checked by a doctor," the officer told Dad. "The house was filthy, and the woman was covered with open sores."

The woman came out of the house and approached the Bronco. David scrambled to the driver's side to close the window and lock the door. She attempted to say goodbye to the children through the closed window, but they just stared at her sullenly from the safety of my lap.

She went to the clothesline and took off the grubby-looking wash and brought it back to Dad.

"I can't have children of my own, and I thought I would get to keep these ones," she told him. She was crying, and although Dad was a compassionate man, I did not hear it in his voice as he said, "And you only had them for a short time. Think of what you put their mother through!"

Dad thanked the officer for his help. He was chomping at the bit to put as many miles as possible behind us before four o'clock. He drove without a stop till 1:00 a.m. before pulling in to a motel to rest and clean up the little ones. Not one complaint had we heard from our hungry, smelly little waifs—Mommy's lap was all they needed.

When it was all over, Dad's one comment was "Give me a grizzly any day, rather than an unreasonable man!"

But he willingly took the risk—for me and mine.

Chapter Thirty-Two

Lessons on Life

Contributed by Leander Goertzen

Dad was my hero from the time I was little up through adulthood. He knew how to make me feel so important, like letting me wear his helmet or his cowboy hat.

I was three or four years old, and we had been out riding. We had stopped for a rest, and Dad was removing the tack. He handed me the bridle and asked me to hang it on a branch. I took it to a nearby tree and reached way up high to hang it. I guess I lost my balance because the next thing I knew, I had jammed a sharp, dry branch into my arm.

I was big stuff, and without a tear, I walked over to show Dad the stick poking out of my arm. Dad pulled out the stick and then calmly got out his jackknife to remove the splinter that was left. That knife had pulled out many a sliver, but this one must have been rotten, because it broke off deep inside, and I had to go all the way to Merritt to see the doctor. I saved my trophy in a little bottle to show my sisters.

A year or so later, we moved sheep and all to Chase Creek. Dad still had one more load of odds and ends to get from Merritt. Mom had to run in to town for groceries, so he asked me if I'd like to ride to town with him. Why would I turn down an offer like that? I grabbed my sock monkey, and away we went. We waited and waited for Mom at Chase. Finally, Dad realized she must have misunderstood which way he was going, and that's how I got the privilege of riding along on an unplanned trip to Merritt with Dad.

He knew how to turn lemons into lemonade. I got to sleep in his big, cozy sleeping bag. Even more resourceful was the menu. For supper we each had half a cantaloupe. We carefully cleaned out all the fruit and saved the skins to use as breakfast bowls. We ate our cornflakes and milk out of them the next morning.

When Dad worked away from home, our vacation treat was to spend a week with him in the bush. He was falling with Uncle Frank at this particular time, so they took all five of us kids up there: Bonnie, Dianne, Brenda, Jewel, and me. Bonnie and Dianne were the oldest, (probably about twelve and eleven) so they were supposed to do the cooking and watch out for us younger ones during the day. But somehow, war broke out between the two leaders, and it was serious!

The cabin was divided into two zones, even the table, and neither was to cross that boundary. Bonnie claimed Jewel and me, and Dianne took Brenda. We younger ones were mostly interested in having a good time, but of course, we tried to be loyal to our sister.

Lessons on Life

There was a strained cease-fire when our dads came home, but the battle was resumed as soon as they left for work the next morning. This continued for several days. Our dads must have been aware of it, but they wisely did not interfere. They knew it would blow over if the adults didn't start fanning it and taking sides, and it did.

I was about nine, and we were living on the farm at Grandview Flats, near Armstrong. It was Friday evening, and Dad was home for the weekend. There was the smell of freshly baked buns, and all should have been peace and happiness, but it wasn't. It was my turn to dry dishes. Can you believe that with three sisters in the house, such a thing would be expected of me? Disgusting!

Marilyn was washing, and she was doing her best to quietly encourage me to get busy with my towel, but it wasn't working.

Dad called cheerily from the living room, "Sure was a good supper, wasn't it, Johnny?"

That was his way of letting me know that he was aware of what was going on in the kitchen, and Marilyn redoubled her efforts to get me in a cooperative mood.

Finally Dad walked into the room. "Hey!" he said pleasantly enough. "Would you like to go downstairs with me?"

Here was my chance to escape. "Oh, yeah!" In my mind's eye, I thought we were going to look at Dad's power saws. What a trade-off for dishes. I don't know where my head was—It was Friday night—Sabbath. About halfway down the stairs, I realized this was not a good direction to be going, but it was too late. I learned there are worse things in life than drying dishes.

Bonnie and I were working for Dad limbing trees on the Finlay River. We had the little aluminum boat for short runs and the thirty-six-foot riverboat for hauling supplies and for serious trips. Uncle Frank was falling with Dad, so with four of us, plus saws and other gear, we were using both boats to and from our work site.

At the end of this particular day, I thought we could have a little fun. "Let's beat Dad and Uncle Frank home," I said to Bonnie.

We jumped into the twelve-foot aluminum boat, started the 9.5-horsepower Evinrude with a roar, and got off to a good head start. About halfway back to camp, the motor gave a sputter, and before I could switch to the full tank, it gave a cough and died.

We must beat the men to camp, so I jumped up and yanked the cord a few times, when "ROAR!" The boat took off, full throttle, and I found myself in the water as quick as that. Bonnie froze in her seat while the boat crazily circled me.

I made a grab for an edge and hung on for dear life to escape the propellers. Bonnie finally got herself in gear and took charge of the controls. I could have been cut up or drowned. I arrived back at camp somewhat subdued and very soaked.

When the men got home, I shared our story. Dad's only comment was, "Remember, I told you to sit DOWN whenever you start that Evinrude!"

Dad knew how to get along with almost everyone, but I know of at least one exception. Rick was a young, strong know-it-all hired hand on the ranch at Tatla Lake when we arrived. He and Dad did not see eye-to-eye when it came to horses, and it didn't take long to come to a head.

Rick was determined to do his thing, but Dad told him flat out, "NO!" I saw Rick's face turn red, and he took a mighty swing, but Dad saw it coming. He jumped toward Rick, and in the quick scuffle that followed, Rick pinned Dad's arms.

Two of Dad's sayings were "There's more than one way to skin a cat" and "Never say whoa in a bad place." He lived by both. He grabbed Rick by the stomach with his teeth and hung on. Then Dad said through his clenched teeth, "I'll let you go as soon as you agree to get off this ranch."

Rick left. And I gained a respect for a side of Dad that few people ever saw.

Most of the time, we used horses to check on the cattle at the ranch, but when the snow came, we used the tractor more. One cold morning, Dad said, "No tractor today. Let's take the horses."

We bundled up, leaving the saddles off so we could benefit from the horses' body heat. Chief was a half-length ahead of Lady as we trotted along. Dad was talking away.

Suddenly, it dawned on him that I was being unusually quiet. He glanced back at me to discover that although Lady was right there beside him, I wasn't.

I guess Lady got tired of me bouncing up on her neck every time we went downhill, so she dumped me in a snow bank, then kept on without missing a beat.

I figured the joke was on Dad—all that good advice was wasted on a horse.

I had quite a temper. Dad didn't have a problem with anyone's having a temper, so long as it was kept under control.

We were in Celista, and I was driving a skidder for Steve Crombie. Dad and I often worked pretty close together—within hearing distance, I learned.

I guess I was an impatient seventeen-year-old, heady with a well-paying job.

Never Say Whoa In A Bad Place

One day on the way home, Dad said, "You must have been having a lot of fun today."

That took me by surprise. Everything that could go wrong had. I had lost my temper more than once. I kept quiet, wondering where he was going with this.

"I kept hearing you say, 'Fun! Fun! Fun!'" Dad continued without even a glance my way.

I was mortified! I knew that Dad knew what I had really said. There wasn't another word about it. There didn't need to be.

Dad loved a practical joke now and then. One time we were riding home together near Lilloet. The town is down on the Fraser River, and the road down to it is steep, with plenty of switchbacks. Suddenly Dad started pumping the brakes, but the pickup wasn't slowing down, and another switchback was just ahead.

"No brakes," Dad announced. "Hang on!"

Over the bank we went, heading for outer space so far as I could see.

Dad stopped the pickup and laughed. "Wasn't that a good one?"

I certainly couldn't have guessed that there was a trail over that steep bank, but I needed a little more time to see the funny side of my near-death experience.

Chapter Thirty-Three

My Knight in Blue Levis

Contributed by Jewel (Goertzen) Lien

Let's go back to the Wild West part of my life that I shared with Lee, Mom, and Dad at Little Horn Ranch. I had just turned fourteen and Lee was fifteen. This was a place Mom wanted no part of, and she stated firmly that she wasn't going. The fact that Dad returned from his first venture there sporting a nice, bright shiner only increased Lee's and my enthusiasm for the move. This was honest-to-goodness adventure. I'm glad we won out.

We arrived in the summer of 1971 in the middle of a hostile takeover where we (mostly Dad) chased the bad guys off. Thus began the work of putting things back on track at the Little Horn Ranch. Many of the other ranchers in the area wanted little or nothing to do with the place after too many bad dealings with the previous managers.

Dad had such a wonderful way with people, and before long, he had earned the trust of nearby ranchers, making lifelong friends with many of them.

We were located west of Williams Lake in the Chilcotin area of BC, dead center between Tatla Lake and Tatlayoko Lake. Truly, this is some of the most beautiful country you'll find anywhere.

That first summer, Lee invited his friend Bill Rice to come spend a few weeks with us. Fortunately, I had two cousins about my age, Gail and Renee, who also stayed with us. Sure, there were chores, but every day we'd saddle up and go riding over the mountains and along hillside trails. This was the life. We also went fishing! I have not before or since found a better place to fish for dollyvardin or rainbow trout than right there in our little meadow river.

Dad showed me how easy it was to lay on my stomach on one of the rickety little bridges with nothing but a fishing line and a plain old hook. You can't get more basic than that. I'd lie there, jerking my line to drum up some attention. The water was so clear I could see the fish only a few feet away. With no bait, it might take fifteen or twenty minutes for the first bite. After that, it was easy. I would pop out an eyeball and bait the hook with it. In fifteen minutes, I'd have about ten more small fish.

It made great fast food when unexpected company showed up. Without a phone, most of our company was unexpected. Dad showed me how to clean them up and put together just the right spices and flour to roll them in before frying them up.

One evening, we had folks drop in from Vancouver—city folks. I made a mad dash out the back door, onto our little Honda 70 motor-

My Knight in Blue Levis

bike. This was going to be my fastest fishing trip ever! I was back and frying up fish in less than half an hour.

One of the young fellows watched me clean and fry up a few of these little beauties. To his shock and Dad's amusement, the fish were so fresh they began flipping in the pan! I told him I'd just hold the lid on so they wouldn't get away.

Most of my mental pictures of Dad are of him wearing his cowboy hat, whether he was with horses or not. He never stopped wearing jeans and actually looking good in them. He was in great shape, which he contributed to riding horses, claiming that it gave a whole-body workout.

Although he was successful at almost any occupation he put his hand to, he spent most of his adult life as a logger falling trees. You could put a mark on the ground anywhere around a tree, and he could drop it there. Pretty much up to age seventy, he was out there giving the young bucks a run for their money.

One of the great loves of his life was horses. And he was like magic with them. If anyone had a hopeless horse, they could bring it to John.

Dad was definitely an outdoorsman. He is the only guy I know who could live comfortably in a tent outside in sixty degrees below zero temperatures. He could make a spruce-bough bed soft enough to bounce on, and the scent was a wonderful bonus. Not much more than a little flour and a skillet in his pack? How about banuck or flapjacks flipped over a campfire. Lost sheep, cattle, child? He was better than a bloodhound. And stories; he could tell wonderful stories.

When I was twenty-one, I shared some great times with Dad while working with him in a logging camp at Port Hardy. We'd get socked in with bad weather, sometimes for weeks at a time. Stuck in a logging camp out in the boonies brings you back to basics. We had a lot of time to talk and laugh.

Flying in those little planes up and down the coast brought me closer to Dad and also to God in the trust department.

On one trip home, we were traveling about ten thousand feet up. We were flying through beautiful clear skies as we headed over the coastal mountains toward Vernon. I could see for miles.

Without warning, the plane's engine sputtered and died. I cannot tell you how very quiet that was! The pilot pulled back hard on the wheel to keep the nose of the plane up. It held for a moment, and then plummeted downward.

I looked out far below at the snowcapped mountains and small lakes, wondering how this plane could be brought down without us dying. Would it be better to try the water or the snow?

The pilot was frantically trying to figure out what had gone wrong with this unfamiliar plane when he found the switch to the second fuel tank. Just like that, the plane fired up, and we regained altitude again.

Dad and I had been dead silent up to that point. But now I found my lungs and began hollering, "I want off this plane right now!"

Dad laughed and suggested we thank the Lord instead. So we did.

At the end of his life, I remember sitting alone beside my tired Dad. He was drifting from one morphine-filled dream to another. For a brief moment, he woke up, gave me a small smile, and tried to speak. I told him that I loved him. I treasured this time alone with him, holding his big hand in mine. I prayed, knowing that my Forever Friend was close. That comforted me.

Dad drifted off again and snored lightly, like he did on the couch

My Knight in Blue Levis

at home. I wished he would wake up and say, "Boy, that was a good snooze!" But that was not to be this time.

As I sat there, I thought about the picture of me as a baby standing on his hand. He always said that I would be the best horse rider with that balance.

What a privilege and honor to be here for him—such a small return for all the times he was there for me.

Christmas morning had barely broken. I was just preparing to leave for the hospital when I got the call that it was over. For a moment, I was a frantic little child who didn't know how I could ever live without him. But God gave me a peace that can only come from Him.

Because I was able to trust my father here on earth, it has made it so much easier to trust my Father in heaven.

We invite you to view the complete
selection of titles we publish at:

www.LNFBooks.com

or write or email us your praises,
reactions, or thoughts about this
or any other book we publish at:

TEACH Services, Inc.

P.O. Box 954
Ringgold, GA 30736

info@TEACHServices.com

www.ingramcontent.com/pod-product-compliance
Lightning Source LLC
Chambersburg PA
CBHW070549160426
43199CB00014B/2434